HENRY MARTEN

and the

LONG PARLIAMENT

Henry Marten

and the

Long Parliament

By IVOR WATERS

"Henry Marten is a tight little fellow, though of somewhat loose life; his witty words pierce yet, as light-arrows through the thick oblivious torpor of the generations; testifying to us very clearly. Here was a right hard-headed stout-hearted little man, full of sharp fire and cheerful light; sworn foe of Cant in all its figures, an indomitable little Roman pagan if no better."

Carlyle: *Oliver Cromwell.*

The Chepstow Society,
41, Hardwick Avenue,
Chepstow, NP6 5DS

ISBN   0   900278   18   8

Printed in Great Britain by
F. G. Comber,
2 St. Mary Street,
Chepstow.

ACKNOWLEDGMENTS

I should like to thank all the librarians and archivists who have enabled me to consult books and documents, and particularly Mr. E.D. Pollard, Monmouthshire County Librarian; Mr. W. John Collett, Newport Borough Librarian; Mr. Geoffrey Dart, Cardiff City Librarian, and Mr. T.J. Hopkins of the Research Room; and the staffs of the above-mentioned libraries and of the British Museum, the Brotherton Library of the University of Leeds, the Leeds-Sheepscar Library, the Berkshire Record Office, the Reading Public Library, and the Buckinghamshire County Library. I am grateful to the Trustees of the British Museum for allowing me to publish engravings and to Mr. Bryan Woodfield for the cover design. I should also like to acknowledge the help given by Mr. F.G. Comber during the production of this book.

Henry Marten
and the Long Parliament

I

For a few years before the execution of Charles I there was a
period of ideological turmoil unmatched until the 20th. century.
During those years Henry Marten was a leader in Parliament
and also in the radical groups not directly represented in the
Commons. His name was as well-known as Cromwell's, but
his reckless championship of new ideas and his opposition first
to the King and later on to the Lord Protector toppled him from
the history books.

His boldness and cheerful disposition made him many friends,
but the royalists knew him as their most uncompromising
opponent, and orthodox members of his own "party" regarded
as an embarrassment a man so notorious as a "lewd liver who
cared little for religion" and who dared to speak out in a Puritan
Parliament for tolerance for Catholics and Jews. Although he
inherited a fortune, he was one of the few members of Parliament
who openly supported the Levellers. He was the first English
republican, and when he expressed his novel opinions in the House
of Commons, he was sent to the Tower by horrified members who
shortly afterwards accepted his ideas as unavoidable.

Henry Marten (generally called Harry) was born in Oxford in
1602 in a house opposite to Merton College church. His father
was an ambitious lawyer who moved to London, where he
started with an annual income of £40 and rose to be head of
his profession, prominent in Parliament, and a favourite of James
I. He was knighted as Sir Henry Marten on January 16, 1616-7
and made Judge of the Admiralty Court in the following October.
He was also Judge of the Prerogative Court for the probate of
wills, so that the King was able to joke that Sir Henry "was a
mighty monarch by sea and land; over the living and the dead".

Harry Marten was sent to a grammar school in Oxford and later to University College as a gentleman commoner. He left with a degree of Bachelor of Arts on January 24 1619-20 and went to the Inner Temple to study law, probably to complete his education rather than with any intention of following his father's profession. One of Harry's enemies remembered many years later: "When a lad you lived in Aldersgate street, under the tuition of the then called 'blue-nosed Romanist' your father, who was the best civilian of our horizon.". John Aubrey says Harry travelled in France, but not Italy. "He was a great lover of pretty girles, to whom he was so liberall that he spent the greatest part of his estate...When he had found out a married woman that he liked (and he had his emissaries, male and female, to look out) he would contrive such or such a good bargain, 20 or 30 li. per annum under rent to have her neer him".

Probably in 1636, when Sir Henry was a very old man and no doubt anxious about the legitimate succession, a marriage was arranged between his son and Margaret, the widow of William Staunton, a rich London grocer. This lady was the daughter of the first Lord Lovelace and the sister of the second. Through his marriage to Margaret Staunton Harry aquired a number of aristo-cratic relations, including Sir George Stonehouse, M.P. for Abing-don, John Wildman, Thomas Lord Wentworth, and Lord Morley and Mounteagle. His dislike of lords was of earlier origin. Acc-ording to Aubrey, Harry Marten married Margaret "somewhat unwillingly, and therefore afterwards living apart from her and following other creatures, she was for some time distemper'd". In spite of this they had five or six daughters and one son.

It was an autocratic age, so the Puritan opposition to the bishops and their ritual was interpreted as resistance to the state. When some of the bolder members of Parliament wanted to make grants of money depend upon a settlement of grievances, Charles I warned : "Remember that Parliaments are altogether in my power for their calling, sitting and dissolution; therefore, as I find the fruits of them to be good or eveil, they are to continue, or not to be". He tried to raise money by a personal levying of tonnage and poundage, and when that failed to satisfy his needs he was forced to call a Parliament in 1628. Sir Henry Marten was one of the members who tried to bring about a reconciliation. "Let us endeavour to breed in the King rather an apprehension of our

A portrait stated to be of Henry Marten hung in the dining-room
at St. Pierre, near Chepstow, until the present century. The above
engraving of part of it was made for Coxe's *Monmouthshire* in
1800.

Coll. John Lilborne.

John Lilburne from *A Remonstrance of Many Thousand Citizens*,
July 7th 1646, probably written by Henry Marten, Richard Overton
and William Walwyn.

general care than any private passion." When Charles realised his demands were not going to be satisfied, he dissolved Parliament and did not call another for eleven years.

During this time he depended upon the support of the law courts. As Sir Henry Marten dominated these and increased his fortune considerably, it is clear that he did nothing likely to make himself a martyr. His fortune grew by good business management and some curious transactions. In 1628 Charles I claimed the estate of a bastard named Bowdler, but it was alleged, "The judge of the Prerogative Court, Sir Henry Marten, hath got almost all the personal estate". On February 16 1628-9 there was a petition against Sir Henry "for converting a great part of the personal estate of one Browne, who died worth £50,000". He became a big landowner, acquired Longworth in Berkshire and, in 1633, bought the manor of Becket, near Shrivenham, in the same county.

He bought more and more land, yet Sir John Lambe was writing to Archbishop Laud on March 21 1638-39 that Sir Henry Marten had no money: "One son spends his £1,000 per annum, the other £500, and he builds churches, gives flagons, keeps house, and marvels that it can be thought he has any." When Laud and Charles I tried to force the English liturgy into Presbyterian Scotland, Sir Henry lent the King £3,000, but Harry excused himself from contributing towards the Scots War on the grounds that he had otherwise assisted his majesty. In fact, the collection of Ship Money had been getting increasingly poorer in Berkshire, with some suspicions that Harry Marten was partly responsible.

In 1640 the Earl of Strafford raised an Irish army and advised the King to call a parliament to provide help against the Scots. By this time the Puritans had grown in numbers and influence. Their leaders, John Pym and John Hampden, had resisted Charles's autocratic demands for many years, but still believed the King had been misled by his advisers, particularly by the bishops. Pym began to negotiate with his fellow-Presbyterians, the Scots, and Charles replied by dissolving the Short Parliament he had recently called. On July 5 he seized bullion worth £130,000 which the Spanish government had sent to the Tower to be coined. The financial crisis encouraged the Scots to cross the border, and 25,000 men under Alexander Leslie seized Newcastle. The King was forced to surrender, promise to pay the

Scots £850 a day for expenses, grant them Northumberland and Durham as security, and call another English Parliament.

Harry Marten was a member of the Short Parliament and he was again nominated for Berkshire later the same year. He had had every opportunity to learn about politics in his father's household, but until 1640 people who did not know him well thought he had wasted his wit and intelligence and his father's money on wine women and song. Anthony à Wood said, "He was a man of good natural parts, was a boon familiar, witty, and quick with repartees, was exceedingly happy in apt instances, pertinent, and very biting; so that his company being esteemed incomparable by many, would have been acceptable to the greatest persons, only he would be drunk too soon, and so put an end to all mirth for the present. He was as far from a puritan as light from darkness. His stature was but midling; his habit moderate; his face not good."

What did such a man have in common with John Pym? They both saw the House of Commons as the most important means of government and they both disapproved of bishops, though for different reasons. After the King's agreement with the Scots, Pym rode from town to town to rouse support for Puritan candidates, and Harry probably enjoyed himself as usual. According to Aubrey, the King was going to watch a race in Hyde Park and, seeing Marten walking there, said loudly, "Let that ugly rascal be gonne out of the park, that whoremaster, or els I will not see the sport". He left, but remembered the King's words. "That sarcasme raysed the whole countie of Berks against him."

II

The Berkshire county election was held at Abingdon on October 26 1640, and Henry Marten was re-elected as one of two knights of the shire. For eleven years Charles I had ruled as an autocrat with the help and advice of bishops, lords, and judges, and even when it was obvious he depended upon the goodwill of Parliament for money, he still believed in his own right to absolute power. Most members of Parliament could not imagine the King could be wrong except as the victim of wicked advisers, and therefore they arrested the two they considered most guilty - Thomas Wentworth, Earl of Strafford, on November 11th. and Archbishop William Laud a month later. Pym accused Strafford of high treason, of undermining the laws of the country and the authority of Parliament, and of advising the King that "he had an army in Ireland which he might employ to reduce this Kingdom". Strafford replied that by "this Kingdom" he meant Scotland. As for treason, that was possible only against the King and in any case two witnesses were necessary to prove this. The only witness was the elder Sir Henry Vane, whose notes had been destroyed by the King's orders. His son had taken a copy of the notes and passed them on to Pym, but there was still not much likelihood that Strafford could be impeached.

On February 3rd. Henry Marten proposed that Parliament should buy off the Scots with £300,000. Sir Simonds d'Ewes wrote in his diary, "I was much satisfied to hear the sound of that little bell below that named but £300,000 for I at first feared that the demand would have been greater." On March 20th. the Scottish Commissioners were still demanding payment. By this time the House was angry because of the delay in bringing Strafford to trial, and Marten decided to "urge forward the Lords by the threat of bringing the Scottish army" upon them. He moved in committee that the "House could not make any advancement of monies to any purpose until justice were done upon the Earl of Strafford". As a result he was sent by the Commons to ask the Lords for a joint meeting, but returned with the reply that the

Lords had given Strafford further time to answer the charges "maugre the Commons". There was a long debate about the word *maugre*, which some members considered to be disrespectful to the Lords. D'Ewes wrote at the time: "Mr Martin saide, That it was nott a time to thinke of doing businesse, neither to day nor to morrow: nor, till the Lord Strafforde bee tryed, which since the Lords have protracted to another weeke, he could not call it a denyall of Justice, but a delay of Justice, and in some cases a delay is a denyall: and further saide that they had done it maugre the conference. Alsoe, if a poore rogue bee taken butt the day before the Assizes, hee shall be tryed the next day; and is asked if hee bee guiltie, nott if he bee readie, and how he will be tryed, nott when he will be tryed".

On April 12th. Strafford was faced with a bill of attainder, which needed no absolute proof. The act was passed in the Commons on April 21st. and in the Lords on the 29th. While it was awaiting the King's signature, the Parliamentary leaders began to fear a coup d'état and a rescue attempt by the army from Yorkshire. They learnt that the Tower was being fortified and that Sir John Suckling was bringing armed men into the City. Pym and his friends decided not to antagonise the King by protesting against breach of privilege, but Marten was not satisfied and moved a protestation openly in the Commons. The House appointed a select committee to draft the document which was approved of by Lords and Commons, "and to this the leaders would not oppose themselves, though they conceived it to be improper at that time". Aware that he had advanced as far as members could tolerate, Harry declared, "We are honest, disjointed fellows. Let us unite ourselves for the pure worship of God, the defence of our King and his subjects in all their legal rights".

On May 10th. the King went back on his word to protect Strafford and gave his royal assent to the death warrant. Strafford said, "Put not your trust in princes," and on May 12th. he was beheaded.

Parliament passed acts by which it was to meet at least every three years, and forbidding the dissolution of the present Parliament without its own consent. It replaced the Star Chamber and the regional and ecclesiastical courts by the Common Law and impeached a number of people who had helped the King to erode parliamentary functions. One of the judges fined was Sir Henry

Marten. He died soon afterwards on September 26, 1641, aged 81, and was buried in his manor of Longworth.

Harry inherited his father's estates during the parliamentary recess, and it was said "the whole county of Berkshire rang with the festivities of the Vale of the White Horse; and his personal courtesies to all classes of men gave him unprecedented popularity there". About the same time he publicly tore in pieces the King's commission of array at Longworth and "forbad the people to stand bare at the sessions to do fealty to their lords". The wearing of hats in the presence of authority became symbolical, and a few years afterwards John Lilburne and the Levellers attached very great importance to it.

In September and October there was a terrible massacre of Ulster Protestants, partly due to nationalist resentment against English settlers. The Puritans sympathised with the Irish Protestants and by a chain of thought, via the Queen's court and Roman Catholicism, linked the King with the atrocities. Pym drew up a Grand Remonstrance detailing the illegal acts done by the King and the reforms being carried out by Parliament and this was narrowly carried after a bitter debate. On Dec. 21 a Puritan Council was elected for the City of London and soon afterwards the King dismissed the Parliamentarian Lieutenant of the Tower and tried to arrest the five Puritan leaders, Pym, Hampden, Holles, Haslerig and Strode.

On January 7th. Henry Marten's bill for the confirmation of the subject's liberties in their persons was given its second reading. On January 31st a crowd of 15,000 poor people brought a petition to Westminster calling on Parliament to "suppress the adverse party" and to send help to Ireland. The following day a large crowd of women brought another petition complaining of their poverty caused by the decay of trade. Henry Marten moved that this petition be read to the House and John Pym went out to thank the women for their support.

In February an act was passed expelling the bishops from Parliament. About this time Edward Hyde (who later became Earl of Clarendon) recorded that he was on friendly terms with Pym, Hampden, Marten and Nathaniel Fiennes, and that the latter told him "if the King resolved to defend the bishops, it would cost the kingdom much blood, and would be the occasion of as sharp a war as has ever been in England." Two days later Hyde met Marten, "with whom he lived very familiarly," and remarked that he could not understand Henry's association with the Puritans, "for he did not think him to be of the opinion, or nature with those who governed the House". Henry replied that he "thought them knaves; and that when they had done as much as they intended to do, they should be used as they had used others". Hyde pressed Marten to explain what he meant, and after a pause Henry answered, "I do not think one man wise enough to govern us all." This was the first open avowal of republicanism, but the time to say this in Parliament itself had still not arrived.

The Queen crossed to the Continent, taking the crown jewels to raise money to buy arms, and both sides hurried to seize control of the county powder magazines. In April 1642 Charles I tried to enter Hull, but the Parliamentarian governor refused him admission. In June the King announced that he would pardon everybody except twelve members, including Henry Marten. He tried to get control of the fleet, so on July 4th. the Lords and Commons appointed a committee of safety consisting of Lords Northumberland, Essex, Pembroke, Holland and Saye, and ten members of the Commons, Pym, Hampden, Fiennes, Holles, Waller, Stapleton, Meyrick, Pierpoint, Glyn and Marten.

The King tried to divide the opposition on August 12th. by declaring that his quarrel was not with Parliament, but with particular men "who first made the wounds, and will not now suffer them to be healed." He named his opponents as Lord Kymbolton, Pym, Hampden, Holles, Haslerig, Strode, Ludlow, Venn and Marten. He professed willingness to negotiate but pointed out that Henry Marten had said publicly and unreproved "that the happiness of the kingdom did not depend on his majesty or upon any of the royal branches of that root". On August 22nd. the King decided that the time had come to teach Parliament a lesson, and set up his standard at Nottingham.

The resulting civil war was more complex than earlier dynastic struggles, and one of the few clear facts about it is that men fought bitterly on both sides, though not always for the same reason. The King, the upper classes, and the members of Parliament decided other men's allegiances, and even partisans supported one side or the other because they preferred it *on the whole*, without necessarily agreeing with all its orthodoxies. Members of Parliament were not true representatives (even to-day a small number of active party members choose a candidate for the majority to support, and a lawyer or landowner may become the spokesman for a constituency of factory workers). Local influence was strong, and religious and class differences swayed many people. Others had simply lost patience with the dictatorial Charles I, but only a few like Henry Marten imagined there could be any form of government other than by a king.

If the Earl of Essex, as Captain-General of the Parliamentary forces, had attacked Charles vigorously, he could probably have ended the war very quickly. As it was the King marched on London and was only kept out by the efforts of the trained bands. Charles set up winter quarters in Oxford. Parliament petitioned for peace, but also took the precaution of giving army commands to members who could be trusted. Henry Marten was made military governor of Reading, which he was forced to abandon at the beginning of November. When Essex re-captured Reading on April 27th, 1643 he needed an army of 16,000 foot and 3,000 horse. The King was successful almost everywhere before the worst of the winter set in, but most of the Parliamentary leaders were anxious for a compromise and avoided decisive actions. Essex delayed in Windsor, and on December 5th. Henry Marten stood up in the House to describe the royalist victories all over England and attack the dilatory Captain-General who, he alleged, "would have it was summer in Devonshire, summer in Yorkshire, and early winter at Windsor".

III

Both sides did all they could to raise money and strengthen their forces. The King took contributions by force wherever his army had the upper hand. Parliament "sequestered" the property of gentry who helped the King and later allowed Royalists to redeem their estates for a proportion of their value in cash. The wealthy Puritans were still reluctant to defeat the King, and again negotiated for a compromise at Oxford. The King's final terms were so unsatisfactory that on April 14th, 1643 both Houses refused to accept them. "Let us not trouble ourselves to send away an answer," said Henry Marten, "but rather answer them with scorn, as being unworthy of our further regard."

A letter written by the Earl of Northumberland while he was negotiating with the King fell into Marten's hands, and Henry opened it to see whether it contained any evidence of treachery. On April 18th. the Earl met Harry at a conference in the Painted Chamber and, according to different eye-witnesses, either cudgelled him or struck him over the head with his cane. Swords were drawn by friends of the two parties, but "the Lords could not defend the blows and the Commons could not defend Marten's conduct," so the matter was dropped. By this time there was great mistrust of the King and a good deal of animosity felt by both Houses for each other.

Parliament ordered the sheriffs of London and Middlesex and the Committee for the Militia to remove the Capuchins from the Queen's palace at Somerset House and send them to France. The Committee was also ordered to demolish "superstitious monuments" in the chapel under the supervision of Marten, Gourdon, and Sir Peter Wentworth. Many of the aristocratic Puritans and wealthy merchants were beginning to fear that some members of the Commons would not be willing to halt political changes or accept a Presbyterian national church. When Henry Marten wanted to arm the people to make Parliament's authority supreme, Pym and his friends declared that this would lead to "the utter subversion of this monarchy and the dethroning of the King." On May 1st. Pym moved the appointment of a committee to go

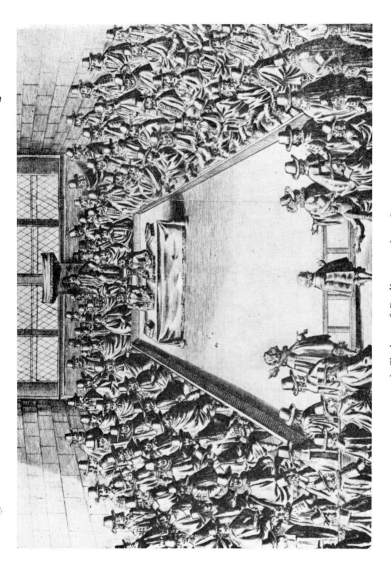

A Sitting of Parliament in 1649.

Execution of Charles I. Engraving by Sebastian Furck, Frankfurt, 1650.

to Scotland to ask for help from the powerful Scottish army, but Marten objected that Parliament ought to assume sovereign authority before sending ambassadors to contract an alliance. When some members argued that it would be useless to ask for help without offering the Scots something in exchange, Henry Marten stood up and, possibly remembering his recent cudgelling, suggested giving them the counties of Northumberland and Cumberland.

A Parliamentarian named De Luke broke open the royal stables on May 3rd. and took two horses. When he was ordered by the Lords to return them he produced a warrant from Henry Marten. Harry told the Lords, "We have taken the King's ships and forts, and may as well take his horses, lest they might be employed against us." The Lords threatened to write to the Lord-General to recall Marten's commission, whereupon the Commons voted that Harry "did very well in not delivering the two horses" and that he should keep them.

Shortly afterwards Marten was ordered by Parliament to seize the royal regalia. On June 2nd. the Commons considered what should be done if the Dean of Westminster refused to give up the keys of the repository, and it was decided by 56 votes to 37 that the door should not be broken open. On the following day it was decided by 42 votes to 41 that it should. There are several accounts by opponents of what happened. The newsbook *Mercurius Aulicus* for June 7th, 1643 reported: "Master Martin and a rabble forced entrance into the Abbie Church at Westminster... brake open two doors which open into a private roome, where the Regalia...have been accustomably kept. But because there was another dore, which must first be opened before they could obtain their entrance, Master Wheeler (whose wife is the King's Laundress) and Falconbridge, Sir Robert Pye's servant in the Treasury, who living long in and about the Close of Westminster had been made acquaint with the secret, by drawing up a beam which made fast that doore...gave him way to enter." According to Peter Heylin, the party broke open an iron chest and took out the crowns, robes, swords, and sceptre, and Marten said "there would be no further use of those toys and trifles." He then dressed George Wither, the poet, in the royal robes, and Wither "being thus crown'd and royally array'd (as right well became him) first marcht about the room with a stately garb, and afterwards with a thousand apish and ridiculous actions, exposed those sacred ornaments to contempt and laughter." *Mercurius Aulicus* added that the Earl of Holland and some members of both Houses arrived and persuaded "the rout to suspend their purpose." Harry, displeased, sealed up the doors. His companions said they would take the crown to give to the King's youngest son, the Duke of Gloucester, but Marten turned on them and said "they were a company of fooles to talk of having crownes and kings, of which there was to be so little use in the times to come."

At the beginning of June the Countess of Rivers obtained a pass from the Lords to allow her to go beyond seas. *Mercurius Rusticus* reported on June 10 that Harry Marten, "plunder-master general, he that so familiarly speakes treason, and steales the King's horses," took the countess's coach-horses in spite of the warrant. "When this warrant was produced to stave off this Parliament horse-taker, he replyed, that if the warrant had been from both Houses he would obey it as coming from the highest authority in England, (sure this man was borne with treason in his mouth) but since it came *but* from the Lords he did not value it: when this warrant could not prevail, the Countess obtaines a warrant from the Earle of Essex to have the horses restored unto her againe, but Mr. Martin to overbeare all, procures an order from the House of Commons to keep them." On June 12th. the House appointed a committee to look into the requisitioning of horses, and a month later referred to another committee "the consideration of the state of Colonel Marten's regiment, what disbursements he has made in raising and keeping of them; and to make him satisfaction; and to employ them for the service of the state."

Sir Simonds d'Ewes noted in his diary on June 26th: "But it is probable that most of the commanders in the saied Earles armie desired not an end of the warre, but a continuance thereof...Mr. Pym moved that Colonel Henry Martin (that notable fierie spirit) might speedilie repaire to his Excellencie the Earle of Essex and if hee had not his whole Regiment of Horse readie nor could instantlie goe himselfe, yet that at least those horses wh weere collected might bee." Harry asked for time to complete his force, no doubt preferring to remain in London to organize activity instead of being absorbed into the inertia of the Lord-General's army.

All through July Marten and his friends urged that Essex should be replaced by Sir William Waller. On July 18th. the Lord Mayor and Common Council of the City petitioned for all forces to be placed under the command of the committee for the militia, which in effect meant the removal of Essex. Two days later thousands of people asked for a *levée en masse* to be led by a Parliamentary committee of thirteen, including Henry Marten. This committee would have power to appoint its own commander-in-chief, and the new army would of course be a political asset to those who raised it. On July 25 *A Memento to the Londoners* declared: "The Kings Forces are growne strong and powerfull, and will in short time, if you prevent it not, be as able to execute their malice upon you as they are willing...The hopes they have swallowed, and brags they have made of pillaging and ransacking this City, may sufficiently inform you what mercy you are like to find when they come amongst you." Henry Marten made at least two reports to the Commons from the Committee of Thirteen urging that they all rise together as one man under Waller. Three important speeches were made on July 28th, one by the Earl of Manchester proposing that all forces should be commanded by Waller; one by Pym attacking the King's latest proclamation; and one by Marten urging a general rising to "take downe the partition wall betwixt well-affected, and ill-affected." "I am of opinion," he said, "that either you must goe forth all, and meete the Enemy as Vassalls with Ropes about your neckes, or like men with swordes in your hands."

There were rumours that Harry Marten was to be asked to command the popular forces. But this Committee for the General Rising lacked money and depended upon voluntary enlistment. It was the International Brigade of the Civil War. The London Militia Committee had the wealth of the City behind it and was able to offer so much better terms than Marten that the general rising attracted only about 300 volunteers. In the end Parliament agreed that Waller should take charge of all forces raised in the City, though still under the supreme command of Essex, and so made certain that there would be no separate command for the Committee of General Rising.

IV

By the middle of 1643 Henry Marten's republican views were well known. *Mercurius Aulicus* reported on May 26 : "It had been rumoured two or three daies before, and was now confirmed, that Master Martin (whose part it seems to be on this publicke Theatre, to bolt out all those dangerous propositions, in which the sense and inclination of the House must first be founded, before they come to be considered of in a formall manner) moved not long since to have His Majesty deposed, as being unserviceable and unusefull in their Commonwealth." On July 16th. the same newsbook stated that Essex had announced he would not fight if the King refused to accept the Treaty of Oxford and that some members of the Commons replied that they could find a better man in that event. "Master Martyn (out of his wonted care of His Majesties safety) was offended at it : saying that if the King would not withdraw, but put his finger to be cut, they could not helpe; what was that to them?"

An army chaplain named Saltmarsh was brought into the House of Commons on August 16th. after papers had been found in his trunk with the words : "If the King would not grant their demands, then to root him out and the royal line, and to collate the crown upon somebody else."

Saltmarsh confessed he had written those words, and there was a proposal to commit him. Henry Marten, who agreed with Saltmarsh except for the suggestion that the crown should be given to somebody else, stood up and said he could not see why the destruction of one family should be put in the balance with the destruction of the whole kingdom. Pym attacked Marten for his immoral life, seeing an opportunity to break the Committee for a General Rising, and since most members could not imagine a government without a king they voted to expel Henry and imprison him in the Tower. "And the tru and onlie cause why hee was at this time putt out of the house," wrote d'Ewes, "was, by reason of the almost constant opposing & often wittilie working at old John Pym."

But Marten's friends were influential and active too, and on

August 19th. the Commons allowed him the liberty of the Tower and access to his papers, and on September 2nd. discharged him altogether without any fees to the gaoler. This short spell in the Tower made Harry a martyr for democracy, and there were many Londoners who wanted to put him in charge of the City forces. But the Presbyterian establishment tolerated no opposition and had already forced the Committee for the General Rising to hand over its funds. On September 25th. Parliament agreed to the "Solemn League and Covenant" to establish the Presbyterian religion in England, and in return for this undertaking and a down payment of £100,000, the Scots undertook to send an army of 20,000 men to support Parliament. John Pym died on December 6th. and it became possible for Marten to be employed again in the army. Anthony à Wood said that for a couple of years he "did good service, first as Governor of Aylesbury and afterwards in command of the infantry at the siege of Donnington Castle."

He was appointed Governor of Aylesbury on May 22nd, 1644, and found the troops "in such want of pay that they are like to disband." On June 18th. he received £300 "on account" and somehow held the garrison together, in spite of lack of money and quarrelling among the troops. Meanwhile, Oliver Cromwell, who had entered Parliament in 1640 with no military experience, had trained his Ironsides so well that he defeated the Royalists at Marston Moor on July 2nd. and so secured the north of England for Parliament. This victory was followed by troop movements in all the towns near the King's capital at Oxford. It became particularly important for Parliament to take Newbury, but after an indecisive battle on October 27th. the King was able to carry off his artillery and leave Sir John Boys in Donnington Castle to offer a most stubborn resistance. Cromwell wanted to attack vigorously, but the Earl of Manchester would not agree, saying "hee was against fighting, giving this as his reason and saying if wee should beate the king never soe often, yet he would be king still and his posterity; but if hee should beate us but once, we must be hanged." Cromwell brought charges against Manchester in Parliament, and the Earl was ordered to return to Newbury and take Donnington Castle.

Sir John Boys resisted all attempts to dislodge him. Henry Marten and his troops were at various times at Aylesbury, Farnham and Abingdon, where Prince Rupert's men wounded one of

Henry's captains. At the beginning of 1645 Aylesbury received reinforcements in the form of 600 dragoons, and Marten remained there for most of that year. For a time the war was less important than the struggle which was going on in Parliament between the Presbyterians and a smaller group of Puritans now becoming known as the Independents, because they accepted each congregation as a Christian unit on its own. Since the Independents were a minority, they believed in a limited degree of toleration, so although Henry Marten was commonly alleged to "care little for religion" he had to attach himself to some group in order to survive, and therefore chose the Independents as being the more tolerant. His enemies said he had more need of tolerance than other men.

On April 3rd. the Independents were able to persuade Parliament that nobody could properly carry out the duties of a soldier and member of Parliament at the same time, and as a result Essex, Manchester and Waller were replaced by Sir Thomas Fairfax and regular officers. The post of Lieutenant-General and leader of the cavalry was given to Cromwell, in spite of the so-called Self-Denying Ordinance. A New Model Army based on Cromwell's Ironsides was enlisted and trained, and on June 14th. this defeated the Royalists at Naseby in Northamptonshire. Here the King's correspondence fell into the hands of Fairfax and, although he was too impressed by the idea of royalty to open it himself, the letters were shortly afterwards read in the Guildhall to members of Parliament and citizens. It was clear from these letters and from others captured later that the King never intended any of his concessions to be binding.

For some time Parliament had been considering the question of electing new members to replace Royalists and to fill vacancies caused by deaths, and on August 21st. agreed to issue writs for elections. One of the members "disabled to sit" was Henry Marten's brother-in-law Stonehouse, who represented Abingdon and joined the King at the end of 1643. Henry took this opportunity to get back into Parliament, and was elected sworn burgess for the borough on October 15th, 1645.

However, in October Cromwell persuaded Parliament to make a strong attack on Donnington Castle. The United forces of Oxfordshire, Berkshire, and Buckinghamshire, with a contingent from Hampshire, were ordered to march to Newbury under the command of Col. Dalbier, with Marten, "being the oldest colonel," commanding on foot. Dalbier found that the houses near the castle had been destroyed, and as there was no cover for a close siege he remained inside Newbury until March. Towards the end of the month Major William Ryves wrote from Donnington describing his attempts to raise a redoubt, when the enemy "who fought like divels" fell on his pioneers and soldiers and drove them back. Ryves continued: "As soon as my men got more Ammunition, having spent their owne on service, I advanced againe to my post, and almost finished the Redoubt ere night. This night Colonel Martin finished it, and drew a line from Dennington Lanes to shelter our approach, and this night or tomorrow we plant our Cannon and great Mortar." In fact, the great mortar with a bore of about fifteen inches caused such destruction that Sir John Boys, learning that the King could not send him any help, agreed to surrender the castle on terms. The articles were signed for Col. Dalbier by Col. Marten, Major Ryves, and Major Collingwood on March 30th, and on the following day Sir John Boys and his men marched out "with Cullers flying and Drums beating."

V

Although Marten had been returned as M.P. for Abingdon, some of his opponents objected that "he was a person dead civilly, and could not be restored to life." Sir Henry Vane retorted that this could easily be solved by expunging from the journal the entry recording his ejection. This was done on January 6th, 1645-6, and Henry once more represented Berkshire. To make sure that Stonehouse should not use this as an opportunity to resume his seat as member for Abingdon, the disablement order against him was repeated.

In February the Covenant became compulsory on all Englishmen over the age of 18. Cromwell and the Independents signed reluctantly. Henry Marten subscribed to the Covenant on June 24th. Anthony à Wood said he was "a taker of all oaths...The last of which being by him taken, he would by all means, as the independent gang did, make the covenant an old almanack out of date." Henry accepted the letter of the Covenant in order to survive, but on June 8th. made his views perfectly clear in his pamphlet *The Interest of England Maintained.* "For Hereticks, Schismaticks, Blasphemers, they are words at Liberty bestowed, and may be retorted: That which some judge Heresie and Schisme, others judge sound Doctrine...on the contrary, find a proper Judge in these cases, and you doe something; but that cannot be found without the Indowment of Infallibility, which none in this Kingdome I thinke, pretend to. But grant that a certain Judge did appear, of an unerring Spirit, and certaine detirmination, that could positively, assuredly give sentence upon every opinion, and distinguish which was truth, and which errour...(In which Case, I beleeve the Presbyter opinions and Tenets, would fare as hardly as any other,) yet this appearing Errour and Heresy, are not to be supprest by Power, but by the efficacy of that Spirit... by Reason convinc'd, not by force compell'd, the minde must be alter'd, not the body subdued."

On May 5th. Charles I surrendered to the Scots, who took him to Newcastle and pressed the English Parliament to make peace. Henry Marten wrote to a Scotsman, "A man would think that our brethren of Scotland are not very fond of the King's person, because they do not carry him into his native Kingdome, which they might as easily do, and with as much leave, as they did carry him from Newark to Newcastle. "He and the other Independents considered it was Cromwell's victories and not the Scottish army which had defeated the King, and therefore did not want to pay the Scots more than £100,000. The Presbyterians on the other hand agreed to pay £400,000 and to send commissioners to Newcastle with propositions for peace. These commissioners arrived on July 23rd. with instructions to remain no longer than ten days and to accept nothing short of the full terms, a Presbyterian settlement with parliamentary control of the militia for twenty years. In spite of Scottish advice, the King rejected the terms.

By this time a growing number of people in London were calling for a greater degree of democracy than Parliament was prepared to give. They were soon to become known as the Levellers, and included John Lilburne, Richard Overton and William Walwyn. On July 7th. the Levellers published a pamphlet called *A Remonstrance of Many Thousand Citizens* in which they attacked Parliament for its failure to prevent the outbreak of war, for their half-hearted conduct of the war once it had started, and for the surrender to Presbyterian intolerance. The pamphlet was anonymous, but is considered to have been the work of Overton, Marten and Walwyn.

The *Remonstrance* told Parliament, "Wee are your Principalls, and you our Agents...For if you or any other shall assume, or exercise any Power, that is not derived from our Trust and choise thereunto, that Power is no lesse then usurpation and an Oppression, from which we expect to be freed." The writers went on to say, "Whatever our Forefathers were; or whatever they did or suffered...we are the men of the present age, and ought to be absolutely free from all kindes of exorbitances, molestations or Arbitrary Power."

The *Remonstrance* declared that "the continuall Oppresours of the Nation, have been Kings," yet Parliament continued to beg and entreat Charles I in submissive language to return to his Kingly Office as if he were a god. Now the oppressors were the wealthy men who held power in Parliament. "Nay, yee suffer poor Christians, for whom Christ died to kneel before you in the streets, aged, sick and cripled, begging your halfe-penny Charities, and yee rustle by them in your Coaches and silkes daily, without regard, or taking any course for their constant reliefe." And the *Remonstrance* warned: "Ye have now sate full five yeeres, which is four yeeres longer then wee intended."

The authors of the *Remonstrance* included in their pamphlet a portrait of John Lilburne which had originally been published with the story of his flogging in *The Christian Mans Trial*, but they got the engraver to draw over it the bars of his prison. Lilburne was originally arrested on April 14 for accusing a man named King of betraying another, but this had developed into a long battle with the Lords and a refusal to acknowledge their authority. Lilburne appealed to the House of Commons, which appointed a committee to look into his case under the chairmanship of Henry Marten. This arrangement pleased Lilburne, but he seized every opportunity to make propaganda out of his public appearances. He was a very prickly individual, and Marten said of him, "If there were none living but himself, John would be against Lilburne, and Lilburne against John." Consideration of Lilburne's case dragged on, and more pamphlets passed through the presses.

Two of these were probably written by Henry Marten. *A Corrector of the Answerer* on October 26th. defended the Leveller Thomas Challoner and asked if Parliament were not bound to punish the King if it found him guilty of tyranny, and *Vox Plebis* on November 19th. supported Lilburne and condemned prison conditions. On January 30th 1646-7 Lilburne published *The Oppressed Mans Oppressions declared* in which he wrote: "Tyrannie is tyrannie exercised by whomsoever; yea, though it be by members of Parliament, as well as by the King, and they themselves have taught us by their Declarations and practises, that tyrannie is resistable."

In May 1647 Lilburne addressed his *Rash Oaths Unwarrantable* to Henry Marten, explaining that for a long time he had looked upon him "as one of the great pillars of the Liberties of the Commons," but he was disappointed by his delaying the report. Henry thought of replying with a pamphlet called *Rash Censures Uncharitable:* "I have oftentimes mett my name bespattered in songs , ballads and pamphlets, yet never troubled my head with framing any counter-song, anti-ballad or vindication, till I found Lieut. Col. John Lilburne firing upon Henry Marten." Towards the end of July Lilburne was convinced by Walwyn that Henry had done his utmost, and offered to pay for printing Marten's retort! However, Henry wrote to Lilburne and decided not to print a reply.

VI

On January 30th 1646-7 the Scots handed the King over to Parliament, and the Presbyterian majority began to think the time had arrived to weaken the Independents by sending part of the Army to Ireland. On April 21st. they decided to send the Newcastle Propositions to the King once more, though Marten told Parliament, "The man to whom these propositions shall be sent ought rather to come to the bar himself than to be sent to any more." When news reached London that crowds were flocking to Holmby House near Northampton, where the King had been taken, in order to be touched by him and cured of scrofula, Henry observed, "he knew not but the Parliament's Great Seal might do it as well, if there were but an ordinance for it."

The Presbyterians determined to disband a large part of the Army and pay the soldiers only a sixth of their back pay. When the news reached them, the 20.000 men elected two Adjutators or Agitators from each troop to speak for them. On May 31st. Fairfax announced that the regiments would not be disbanded after all. On the same evening a young officer, Cornet George Joyce, spent some time with Cromwell and Fleetwood discussing a plan to prevent the Presbyterians from removing the King from Holmby. It is not at all certain how far Cromwell encouraged Cornet Joyce, and he later denied that he had consented to the King's removal "if occasion were." Joyce and about 500 men reached Holmby House on June 2nd. and informed the parliamentary commissioners that they had come as protectors because of a secret plan to "steal away the King." Joyce set guards, but found the following day that Colonel Graves, the Presbyterian guardian of the King, had "gone clean away." He discussed the changed circumstances with his men and decided to remove the King from Holmby. Charles I agreed to go with the troops the following morning "even willingly," but when the time came he asked Joyce what commission he had to take him away. After trying to dodge the question, Joyce pointed to his troopers and the King agreed to go to Newmarket. The same day Cromwell gave up his attempts to compromise and joined the rest of the Army.

On June 5th. Cromwell's son-in-law Ireton issued a document which was unanimously accepted as the Army's refusal to disband. Ireton's *Heads of the Proposals* satisfied the Levellers to some extent by offering Charles I restoration on terms: Parliament to control the armed forces for ten years, religious toleration for all except Roman Catholics (who were linked with England's enemies and regarded as bound up with absolutism and persecution), biennial parliaments, and provision for recording dissents in Parliament, which Henry Marten saw as a step towards representative government. But when the King saw the document he refused to accept it, saying, "You cannot do without me. You will fall to ruin if I do not sustain you." Presbyterian mobs invaded Parliament, and the two speakers, Lenthall and Manchester, with eight Lords and 57 members of the Commons, took refuge with the Army.

On August 4th. the Army marched on London and entered Westminster two days later. The former speakers and members of Parliament took their seats again, but the Presbyterians still had a majority. On August 20th. Cromwell had a regiment of cavalry drawn up in Hyde Park while he and other officers who were also members of Parliament went to the House. The threat sufficed to drive out the most prominent Presbyterians, leaving the Independents in control.

On September 6th. Cromwell went to see John Lilburne in the Tower. He explained that the wrongs Lilburne was complaining about would be righted as soon as possible, but that he could not be released until he promised not to "make new hurley-burleys" in the Army. Marten's committee was unable to do anything for the Leveller leader, who wrote to Henry on September 15th. threatening to "see what the private Soldiers of his Excellencies Army, and the Hob-nayles, and the clouted shooes will doe for me." He also made it clear through Royalist prisoners in the Tower that he would be quite willing to support the King if he could get the terms he wanted.

On Sepember 22nd. Marten moved that no more addresses should be sent to the King. He was supported by Col. Rainsborough, Algernon Sidney, Blake, Ludlow and Col. Hutchinson, and opposed by Cromwell, Ireton and Vane. The republicans secured 34 votes against Cromwell's 84. On the following day Marten and Rainsborough opposed another motion to send one last address to the

King, saying Charles was a Jonah who must be thrown overboard if the ship of state was to come safe to port. This time they were defeated by 70 votes to 23.

Republicans in the 17th. century derived their ideas from reading about the ancient Greek and Roman commonwealths, and to most people Henry Marten was out of step with his age. "This viper," wrote Anthony à Wood, "which had been fostered in the bosom of the Parliament, was against the parliament itself, and against all magistrates like a second Wat. Tyler, all pen and inkhorn men must down." On the other hand probably few men had more friends than Harry, and few men took so many risks in those dangerous times to deserve friends.

On October 13th. John Selden spoke in Parliament on behalf of Catholics as believers in Christ, and Marten supported him by asking why Presbyterians were to be liberated if Catholics were to be excluded. Selden was told that Catholics were idolators and Marten that the Catholics, unlike the Presbyterians, had a foreign prince at their head. The next day Selden and Marten returned to the attack, and Henry told the House it was better to have one tyrant abroad than a tyrant in every parish.

David Jenkins, a Royalist judge who had imprisoned men in some of the Welsh counties for taking up arms against the King, was captured and brought before the House of Commons with Sir Francis Butler to answer a charge of treason. He refused to kneel at the bar as directed by Speaker Lenthall and said boldly, "Since you and this House have renounced your duty and allegiance to your sovereign liege lord, you are become a den of thieves, should I bow myself in this house of Rimmon, the lord would not pardon me this thing." The House was in an uproar and without a trial voted the two men to death. No one could have reasoned with the fanaticism on either side, but Henry waited patiently.

The keeper of Newgate was sent for and asked what were the usual days for executions for treason. He said Wednesdays and Fridays. "Then stood up Harry Marten, (the droll of the house) who had not spoken before. He said he would not go about to meddle in their vote, but as to the time of execution he had something to say, especially as to judge Jenkins. 'Mr. Speaker (says he), every one must believe that this old gentleman here is fully possess'd in his head...that he shall die a martyr...for otherwise he never wou'd have provok'd the house by such biting expressions; whereby it is apparent that if you execute him you do what he hopes for, and desires, and where execution might have great influence upon the people, since not condemn'd by a jury: wherefore my motion is, that this house wou'd suspend the day of execution, and in the mean time force him to live in spight of his teeth.' Which motion of his put the house into a fit of good humour, and they cry'd, Suspend the day of execution."

Aubrey says Henry Marten saved the life of Sir William Davenant, the author of *Gondibert*, by reminding the House that according to the Mosaic law sacrifices were required to be pure and without blemish, and that they were sacrificing "an old rotten rascall." Everybody knew how Davenant had lost part of his nose, and there were probably a few laughs which sufficed to lower the tension and save the poet from execution. In a letter to Marten dated July 8th 1652, Davenant wrote, "I would it were worthy of you to know how often I have profess'd that I had rather owe my libertie to you than to any man." The Earl of Rutland also seems to have owed his life to Marten, for we find him writing that "knowing my innocencye and your *integrité*" he is sustained by Henry's friendship, and later, "Whiles I have right and Henrie Martin on my syde I fear no mineurs nor other unjust scandels which are throwne on me."

On October 16 Cromwell and Marten were tellers in favour of a proposal to consider "the manner of the address to be made to the King." Cromwell wanted this speeded up because he believed the King would reject it and so prepare the way for a more moderate settlement; Marten wanted no settlement at all in which the King should take part. A combination of Presbyterians and Independents rejected the motion, and a few days later Cromwell urged the Commons to restore the King as soon as possible.

Charles was removed to Hampton Court and the Army withdrew to Putney. In the church there the General Council of the Army met from October 28 to November 11 to work out a programme for the future. Ireton said "All the maine thinge that I speake for is because I would have an eye to propertie." Only property owners should vote.Even the Agitators and Levellers supported the small merchant against the rich rather than the wage-earner against his employer. Colonel Rainsborough was far in advance of his age when, on October 29, he said "I do think that the poorest man in England is not at all bound in a strict sense to that government that he hath not had a voice to put himself under.

The result of the conference was *The Agreement of the People* which was read at a meeting of the Council on October 29. The Levellers wanted a republic or a constitutional monarchy with biennial parliaments to sit for six months without any control over religion. The Army criticized Cromwell and Ireton for speaking against the vote of no more addresses to the King, and they took offence and walked out.

While the Army Council was deliberating in Putney church, support for the *Agreement of the People* was being organized in the City by the so-called London Agents. John Wildman was probably their contact with the Army and Henry Marten the only supporter from Parliament. Thirteen years later, when Marten was taken to the Tower, a key to the cipher used by the Levellers in 1647 was found among his papers, with symbols for the names of Marten, Walwyn, and Wildman. Although Henry's reckless attacks left him without much support in Parliament, his courage and unchanging support for democracy had made him very popular outside the walls of the House. Parliament was alarmed at the support stirred up by the London Agents and appointed a joint committee to investigate them.

The Royalist *Mercurius Elencticus* reported that papers had been pasted up "in many Churches, and upon severall Gates and Posts throughout the City, inciting the People to rise as one Man" and that a member had reported this to the House. Whereupon Henry stood up and said "he wondered why anybody should move to restrain the people from seeking redress for their grievances, seeing they had as good a right to represent their condition as any man that sat there." Another member asserted he could prove that Marten had met and encouraged over a hundred "desperate sectaries" in a house in London, and he wondered how any member dare discuss public affairs except in the House. Henry indignantly agreed it was true he had met the people mentioned and added that if they were at the door then "he would go out, and both consult and advise with them."

The Royalist newsbooks gleefully spread rumours of breaks in the ranks. *Mercurius Bellicus* reported: "They begin to impeach one another apace...Who would have thought that Martin, that Butterfly, dar'd to have been so sawcy, as to call Tall Tom Fairfax Traytor. Well, for this trick, I would not wish any friend of mine more (after Fairfaxes decease) ever to be a Parliament General." *Mercurius Melancholicus* printed a rumour that Henry was to be hanged. "Martyn is highly taxed in the House, if they do not clip his wings, and make him hop shorter by the head, Ile say my prayers backwards over 'em."

VII

In November 1647 Charles I escaped from Hampton Court to Carisbrooke Castle in the Isle of Wight. The day after the Parliamentary commisioners arrived there with the "address," proposing very favourable terms for reconciliation, the Scottish commissioners turned up and began to negotiate separately with the King. As a result Charles rejected Parliament's terms and on December 26 signed a secret "Engagement" with the Scots by which they undertook to restore him by force in return for a three years trial of Presbyterianism. By signing this document Charles forfeited any claim to be a martyr for the Church.

More and more members were becoming unable to trust the King's word, and on January 11 a resolution drawn up by Henry Marten was carried in the Commons by 141 votes to 92 that no further addresses should be made: "It never yet pleased the King to accept any Tender fit for us to make, nor yet to offer any fit for us to receive." This time Cromwell supported Marten.

The same day Henry published a pamphlet, *The Independency of England*, beginning with the words, "To rectifie, not to upbraid you," in which he told the Scottish commissioners that many former provocations of theirs had been winked at by Parliament, and that no doubt their recent communications would have been too, except that they had remained in England so long that they had apparently forgotten why they had come in the first place. Marten then proceeded to tell them.

The Scots, he said, had been called in against a common enemy who had been defeated, and they were not required to "settle religion," only to give advice. "So long as we needed the assistance of your countrymen in the field," he told the commissioners, "we might have occasion to give you meetings at Derby House, and now and then in the Painted Chamber, it being likely that the kingdom of Scotland might then have a fellow-feeling with us," but "what Englishman soever shall peruse the papers that you have shot in to both house of Parliament, especially into the house of Commons, these last two years, but would as lieve take advice from the king as from you?"

Henry acknowledged the kindnesses Parliament had received from the Scots and said these would be paid for, but he believed "our neighbours did not know how ill we were, till we were almost past cure, and therefore came slowly to us: and that they did not know how well we were, in a year after we had nothing for them to do, and therefore went slowly from us." Marten argued that the two countries had solemnly engaged to help each other against a third party who might have defeated each singly, so a separate peace was not justified. "A wise man will foresee inconveniences before he make his bargaine, and an honest man will stand to his bargaine notwithstanding all inconveniences." He thought there was a more natural way to end a war than by agreement, and that was by conquest. "I think he that playes out his set at Tennis till he win it, makes as sure an end of it, and more fair, than hee that throwes up his Racket when he wants but a stroke of up, having no other way to rook those of their money that bet of his side."

"A King," he continued, "is but one Master, and therefore likely to sit lighter upon his shoulders than a whole Kingdom, and if he should grow so heavy as cannot well be borne, he may be sooner gotten off than they. You shall see a Monsieurs horse go very proudly under a single man, but to be *chargé en crouppe*, is that which nature made a mule for, if nature made a mule at all." As for religion, "You know we did not enquire at all how orthodox your religion was before we vowed to maintain you in it, in the quiet possessing of it (not in the theological truth of it, a business for a university perhaps, not for a kingdom)."

Although Cromwell had supported the motion of no addresses on Jan. 11th, he was suspected by many members of Parliament and by most of the Levellers of being an opportunist. Suspicions grew because of lack of information, and particularly when a bill was introduced in March to give Cromwell lands from the Earl of Worcester's estates in Monmouthshire and Gloucestershire. Cromwell did receive considerable rewards for his services, but he also remitted large sums to Parliament. The Levellers genuinely feared that Cromwell intended to become a dictator, but they were also afraid of a Scottish invasion. So rumours spread that Marten had provided himself with a pistol and dagger to "play the part of Felton" (the assassin of the Duke of Buckingham) because he was convinced that Oliver had sold the people's cause for an earldom and garter. It was also alleged that Henry had suggested "if they must have a monarchy it were better to have Charles and oblige him, than to have him obtruded by the Scots, and owe his restitution to them."

In February, Col. Poyer, the Governor of Pembroke Castle, refused to be replaced by an officer appointed by Fairfax and declared for the King. In April news reached London that the Scots were preparing to invade England. Fairfax decided to march north, and sent Cromwell to suppress the rising in South Wales. On May 11th Cromwell reached Chepstow, which was part of the estates recently granted to him by Parliament, and found the walls lined with musketry. A royalist newsbook reported that Cromwell was mortally wounded there and carried into his chamber to die. In fact he captured the town and leaving Col. Ewer to besiege the castle, marched towards Pembroke. This second civil war was virtually ended by Poyer's defeat by Col. Horton at St. Fagans, but Pembroke held out until July 11th.

The sudden danger revived the strength of the Presbyterians, who were able to pass the Blasphemy Act which had had its second reading as long ago as September 2nd, 1646. This act threatened certain heretics with death and others with imprisonment for life. Henry Marten and many of his friends were Deists or rationalists. A chaplain who later became Bishop of Chichester once wrote to Henry introducing a friend as "an honourer of your little great philosopher Epictetus and you." Anthony à Wood said all Marten "moved for was upon Roman and Greek principles. He never entered into matters of religion but on design to laugh both at them and all morality." Henry Marten himself had written in 1646 and often endorsed this opinion in later years, "By reason convinc'd not by force compell'd, the minde must be altered, not the body subdued." He had no wish to be hanged, drawn and quartered, and decided that for the time being he could be of more service with the Army than in Parliament.

After taking Pembroke, Cromwell marched north against the Scots. At about the same time Henry Marten began raising a regiment of horse in Berkshire with the help of Col. William Eyres, a Leveller who had started his service in Cromwell's original troop. Reports reached London that Henry was taking horses from inhabitants and that he had become "a right Jack Cade, in declaring against Kings, Lords, Gentry, Parliament, Army, all Clergymen and Lawyers, saying further that he can raise six-score thousand men for the maintenance of these Principles."

Several times Parliament ordered Henry to disband his men, return the horses, and attend the House, but he had no intention of obeying, since he intended his troops to be a defence against the Presbyterians as much as against the Scots. Parliament itself then raised a small private force for its own defence, and *Mercurius Pragmaticus* sneered that they were seizing "all horses they can catch about the suburbs." The House discussed "a whole packet of Complaints out of the County of Berks, against...vertuous Harry Marten, the very flower and Creame of our modern Saintship," who was raising all the horse he could catch under his standard bearing the words *For the People.* "He wanted not advocates enough in the House; who, instead of sending Force to reduce him, dismissed the Complaynants with such another slight Order as they made once before, that Hee and Eyres should come up to the House, and submit first to be disbanded by the Committee of the County...which order you shall see Harry take leisure to obey."

In August many members were alarmed because of Henry's "rare doctrine" at the Reading Quarter Sessions, where he told the jury and others present not to stand bare-headed before the bench, because the people were the supreme authority of England. The wearing of hats in the presence of bigwigs was looked upon by the Levellers as a symbol of freedom. Marten told Lord Craven's tenants not to do homage at his Court-Baron, as this was a badge of the Norman conquest. *Mercurius Pragmaticus* reported that thousands had flocked to him and that Harry preached to the Berkshire rustics "in the habit of a Leveller." "Hee hath already forbidden his owne tenants and Souldiers, not to yield him any manner of reverence, or to be subject unto his commands in ought but what shall concern them in the warre; and now having begun to act the second part of Jack Cade, hee goes on very prettily, having already distributed the tithes belonging to one of the parsons at Reading amongst the poor of the parish."

On August 17th, the day Cromwell met the invading Scots at Preston, a pamphlet appeared in London called *Englands Troublers Troubled.* The Presbyterian Clenent Walker ascribed it to the "second Wat Tyler" Henry Marten, and later authorities have concurred. He attacked the House of Lords as the prime corrupters of the Commons, "So that for any good the house of Lords or any part of them have done in all these eight yeares troubles, it had been happy for this Nation, they had all gone at first with the King, as the rest of them did." Because of the Lords' influence the Commons had been corrupted, "and amongst them a plaine man is made the scorn of rich men, yea of Lawyers who are the vilest of men, and greatset abusers of mankind." In the courts, he alleged, jurymen and people were frightened by unjust judges and corrupt lawyers, and men of property were concerned only with increasing their wealth without any sympathy for the poor.

On August 21st, Parliament sent Major Fincher down to Berkshire to suppress Marten, and on the 24th, repealed the Vote of No Addresses to be made to the King. News soon arrived that Harry and his Levellers had gone into Leicestershire where "They will levell all sorts of people, even from the highest to the lowest, and...he that hath the most, shall be equall with him that hath the least." The writer was not a sympathiser, but admitted that Harry had given orders "That no souldier whatsoever shall dare to plunder or use violence against any, but that they behave themselves civilly." He said that if these orders were observed, in all probability the Levellers would grow very numerous, "if not timely suppressed."

On September 11, a petition, alleged by *Pragmaticus* to be of "Harry's own framing" and claimed by the Levellers to contain 40,000 signatures, was presented to the Commons again protesting against any treaty with the King. *Pragmaticus* called it "a most eminent peece of Vilany, and very like the Author of it." The petitioners wanted to take away the negative votes of the King and Peers, to make everybody liable to the law, to take away the power of "pressing men to the warre," to abolish tithes, to cancel the privileges of the City companies, to call the King to account, and to allow "a liberty to that rude Beast, the Plebs, to censure affaires of the highest concernment." The petitioners were centuries ahead of their time, but *Pragmaticus* concluded gloomily, "To this end it is, that Harry Marten took up arms lately, not without private direction from Nol. Cromwell," and when they had finished the work in the north they would come and finish it in the Houses.

VIII

Again Parliament tried to negotiate with the King at Newport, and again Charles pretended to make concessions to gain time. After Cromwell had beaten the Scots he came slowly south. Henry Marten seems to have joined up with him in York. Col. Rainsborough was murdered by two disguised Royalists in Doncaster and Henry probably attended his funeral in Wapping on November 14, when thousands of Levellers took Rainsborough's colour, sea-green, as their badge. The following day a meeting took place between three Independents and three Levellers who agreed that a discussion should take place to try to arrive at a common policy. The Independents, the Levellers, the Army, and the "honest men of Parliament" were asked to choose four representatives who would put their case.

The committee met in the Council Chamber in Windsor Castle, but Marten was the only member who attended from Parliament, because all the others were against a dissolution. Henry and four representatives of the Levellers locked themselves up in their lodgings and completed a second draft of the *Agreement of the People* which proposed dissolution on April 30, 1649, a new Parliament based on householder suffrage, with biennial elections in 300 constituences.

After the arrival of Ireton and the Southern Army, the committee transferred itself to Whitehall. The Levellers made a number of concessions in the hope that the amended *Agreement* would be widely circulated for discussion, but instead it was sent to the Council of Officers. On November 20th, the Army sent Col. Ewer to Parliament with a "Remonstrance" demanding that the "chief delinquent" should be brought to trial and that the soldiers should be paid the arrears of pay owed to them. Parliament took no notice, so the Army sent Ewer to remove the King from Newport to closer confinement in Hurst Castle in Hampshire.

John Lilburne claimed that he told Independents he thought the King was a tyrant, but that it was in the Levellers' interest to balance the King, Parliament, and the Army until they knew for certain which of those tyrants "that pretended fairest would give us our freedoms." Marten evidently also thought like this, as appears from a commission he issued on November 25th, appointing Symon Rice captain over a troop of 80 men in Henry's private army: "Whereas by virtue of that right which I was borne to as an Englishman, and in pursuance of that duty which I owe my said country, I have resolved to raise and conduct a Regiment of Harquebusiers on horse back on the behalf of the people of England, for the recovery of their fredome, and for common justice against all tyranny and oppression whatsoever." Then as now it was hard to define justice and tyranny. On December 2nd. the Commons decided by 129 votes to 83 to come to an agreement with the King, on the grounds that he could now be trusted to make essential concessions, and later the same day the Army leaders and the Independents came to the conclusion that their only hope of securing justice against tyranny was to expel the Presbyterians.

On December 6th, Col. Pride surrounded the Parliament building and turned out the Presbyterian majority. Most of the excluded members left without resistance and about 45 others were placed under arrest for a few days in a nearby tavern popularly known as 'Hell.' On December 7th, Cromwell arrived, disclaiming knowledge of the purge but saying he was glad of it. *Mercurius Pragmaticus* reported with its usual gusto: "The house being thus cleansed, in came that pure holy Goblin Nol. Cromwell, who brought in along with him his Fellow-Saint Harry Marten...and the case of the apprehended Members being reported, how that they had been kept up all night out of bed in the Cooks house called Hell, Harry would needs break a Jest; that since Tophet was prepared for Kings, it was fit their friends should goe to Hell."

The *Agreement of the People* had proposed a dissolution of the House, not a purge. Sir Henry Vane left the Commons disillusioned. Some of the Leveller leaders, including Wildman and Sexby, decided to look after their own interests, and John Lilburne went off to Durham, where he had been given Royalist estates. Henry Marten apparently still had faith in Cromwell or at least in the power of Parliament to restrain him.

Ireton and the Army were impatient to bring the King to trial, but there was no precedent in history and the legal difficulties were enormous. An ordinance to set up a tribunal of three judges and a jury of 150 was rejected by the Lords, and in any case the judges refused to take part. On January 6th, Parliament passed a new ordinance creating a court of 135 commissioners to be both judges and jury, but about half of the men named refused to act. Some people thought it would be better if the King were tried in the King's Bench as an ordinary criminal, others were afraid there would be a popular revulsion against republicanism.

One of the Puritans who had suffered at the hands of the King and bishops, William Prynne, made a long speech in Parliament on December 4th, claiming that the King's offers were now satisfactory and that the Army officers were rebels. He persisted in these attacks, and on January 6th, Marten replied with a pamphlet in which he sympathised with Prynne's sufferings in prison and the cruel loss of his ears, but pointed out that Parliament had brought about his release and given him £5,000 compensation. Prynne, said Henry, had railed against everybody. "This humor of his puts me in minde of a Gentleman that was as nimble with his sword, as this Mr. William with his Pen. It happened that two set upon one; this blade taking pleasure in fighting, draws, and takes part with the single man: now they are two to two. It fell out, that two men, friends to the single man come by, and seeing their friend ingaged, take part with him; the contentious Gentleman seeing that, goes over to the other side, and making them three to three, fights as eagerly as before...Should the Apostles come from Heaven, sent thence to institute a Government, Mr. Prynne would dissent from, and wrangle with them...His business is to write lyes in the Name of the Lord." On January 9th, Parliament considered Henry Marten's report and recommendations for a new Great Seal and ordered that one should be made with the arms of England and Ireland on one side and an engraving on the reverse showing a sitting of the House of Commons, with the words, "In the first year of freedom by Gods blessing restored, 1648." Henry had been reprimanded by Vane for using the word *restored*, whereupon Marten "standing up, meekely replied that 'there was a text had much troubled his spirit for severall dayes and nights of the man that was blind from his mother's womb whose sight was restored at last.' i.e. was restored to the sight which he should have had.

On January 19th, 1648-9 the King was brought from Windsor to St. James's, and his trial began in Westminster Hall on the following day. The Lord President John Bradshaw presided, and about seventy commissioners sat at one end of the court on tiers of benches covered with scarlet cloth. At the back, under the arms of the Commonwealth, sat Oliver Cromwell and Henry Marten. It was alleged at the latter's trial eleven years later that as the King was arriving from the river, Cromwell told the other judges they must be ready with an answer if Charles should ask by what authority they sat, and that Marten gave the reply: "In the name of the Commons and Parliament assembled, and all the good people of England." With these words the charge was made accusing Charles Stuart of High Treason and High Misdemeanours. The King refused to recognise the court, and his dignified conduct at the trial won respect even from many who despised his previous acts of treachery. Charles was able to emerge as the champion of law and Episcopacy, though he had always claimed to be above the law and had professed himself willing to accept Presbyterians to regain his throne. To the Army he was the "man of blood" who had treacherously caused the loss of many lives, and so he was sentenced to death.

Only 28 of the commissioners were willing to sign the death warrant, but Cromwell went round gathering more signatures and in the end collected 59. At Marten's trial a witness alleged that he was in the Painted Chamber on January 29th, and saw parchments with seals upon them. "I did see a Pen in Mr. Cromwell's Hand, and he marked Mr. Marten in the Face with it, and Mr. Marten did the like to him." If they did so, no doubt it was to break the tension of the most memorable decision of their lives. On January 30th, Charles I was taken to Whitehall for execution. Right to the end he insisted that his power was absolute and that he was not accountable to his subjects. His dignified conduct on the scaffold, as at his trial, made people forget his tyrannical rule and bad faith and agree with Charles that "a subject and a king are clean different."

IX

The Royalist newsbooks abused Marten more than ever, but now the House valued his support and on February 2nd, ordered that his regiment of horse should be officially recognized and taken into the regular strength of the Army. It never actually became part of the establishment, but the intention reflected the change in Henry's position.

On February 6th, it was moved in the Commons that "the house of peers in Parliament is useless, dangerous, and ought to be abolished." Henry Marten moved an amendment that the "Lords were useless, but not dangerous," but he withdrew this derisive suggestion and the motion was carried. The few members of the House of Lords that were left adjourned without fuss and did not meet again until 1660. The following day the Commons agreed that kingship had been found by experience to be unnecessary, burdensome, and dangerous to the liberty, safety, and public interest of the people, and accordingly abolished it. The House also agreed to Marten's proposal that the King's statues at the Royal Exchange and other places should be taken down and the following inscriptions placed on the sites: *Exit Tyrannus Regum ultimus. Anno libertatis Angliae Restitutae primo.*

On February 13, Parliament set up a Council of State of 41 members, including Cromwell, Bradshaw, Vane and Marten. Any nine of these members were to constitute an executive to meet at Derby House. Ireton wanted all members of the Council to approve the establishment of the High Court of Justice, the trial and execution of the King, and the abolition of the monarchy and the Lords. Algernon Sidney objected that a test would "prove a snare to many an honest man, but every knave would slip through it." Lord Grey of Groby complained that Sidney had called everybody a knave who had signed this agreement, but Henry soothed ruffled feelings by pointing out that Sidney had simply said "that every knave might slip through, and not that every one who did slip through was a knave." It was then agreed that every member of the Council of State should sign the Engagement proposed by Ireton.

For a short time Lilburne and his colleagues were looked upon by government as friendly fellow-travellers, but the Levellers did not approve of the idea of a Parliament to sit for six months followed by a Council of State to rule for the next eighteen. The Commons soon found that Lilburne was an aggressive individualist, a primitive anarchist disillusioned by the growing conservatism of the Army leaders. The officers tried to prevent the re-introduction of the Agitators and also banned petitions, which were being used as a device to avoid censorship. On March 1st, eight troopers protested on behalf of the rank and file that they were "English soldiers engaged for the freedoms of England and not outlandish mercenaries to butcher the people for pay" and asked, "Is it not the Souldier that endureth the heat and burden of the day, and performeth that work whereof the officers beareth the glory and name?"

The Council of Officers immediately cashiered the troopers and punished five who did not apologize. *Pragmaticus* reported that Lilburne and his confederate, "that pernicious Catiline" Harry Marten, had sent out followers into Hertfordshire, Berkshire, and Hampshire to post up addresses in market-towns and call upon the people to refuse to pay excise and other unreasonable taxes. In this instance *Pragmaticus* was overstating his case.

On March 21st, Overton published a pamphlet called *The Hunting of the Foxes* condemning the treatment of the five troopers. "We were before ruled by King, Lords and Commons; now by a General, a Court Martial and a House of Commons; and we pray you what is the difference?" Overton said the requirement to abstain from politics should apply to officers as well as to men. "You shall scarce speak to Cromwell about anything, but he will lay his hand on his breast, elevate his eyes and call God to record, he will weep, howl, and repent, even while he doth smite you under the fifth rib." The Leveller writers sent in a petition called *Englands New Chains, Part II*, and on March 28th, Lilburne, Walwyn, Overton, and Prince were arrested and sent to the Tower.

Henry Marten was now playing a difficult and devious part, not merely to survive in Parliament but even to continue his criticisms at all. *Pragmaticus* hinted that he was drifting to the "Grandees," but his friends in the Tower did not think so. They asked to be allowed to debate their case with any four men in

England, Cromwell and Ireton to be two of them, "and if we can agree, there is an end, and all our interest, but in case we cannot, let them...chuse any 2 more, *viz* Col. Alex. Rigby and Col. Henry Martin, to be final umpires betixt us, and what they, or the major part of them, determine...we will acquiesce in."

The private career of Marten's regiment was not yet over. On April 19th, Leveller troops, including some from Henry's horse, assembled in Oxfordshire, and the same day the Committee of Wiltshire complained about the "ill carriage of Coll. Martins Regiment in this County; among others this day divers honest men of Whitchurch and places adjacent...express their deepe sence of the greate oppressions and outrages done upon them very lately by those soldiers." On May 7th, a rendezvous of troops at Banbury was joined by most of Marten's regiment, and one of his close friends was involved in resistance at Burford. Here the Leveller soldiers were surprised by Cromwell during the night of May 14-15th, and, although 500 men escaped, 340 were taken prisoners. The last centre of resistance was the Crowne Inn where Col. Eyres fought desperately until taken prisoner. Fairfax and Cromwell ordered a court martial which executed three soldiers as an example to the rest of the prisoners, who were made to watch from the leads of Burford church.

A big estate at Burford was given to Speaker Lenthall, £1,500 was spent on plate and purse to five generals, and £3,500 on wine and food on June 7th, for Thanksgiving Day. This expenditure seems to confirm the accusations made by Clement Walker, one of the ejected Presbyterians, that the Independent Grandees were careerists with houses in the Low Countries "richly furnished with Sequestred Plate, Linnen, and Stuffe." Walker alleged that Pride's Purge had been a deep plot hatched by Cromwell. "Oliver is a Bird of Prey, you may know by his Bloody Beak."

After reading Walker's *History of Independency*, Henry Marten noted: "It is clear to me that a wholl Parliament can have no plott at all; they are so numerous, and so mingled in temper and education, age and intersts, that so great a party as hee calls Independents could not drive on any project of that bulk, so long a brewing, with secrecy sufficient for such an enterprise. And it is not clear to me that the single person you speak of did lay those eggs, or sett a brood upon them, which we see hatched indeed to his advantage. He was a man of a high spirit from the beginning, very active and vigilant; he had got a crew about him of blades that would follow him through any other fire to avoid the fire of persequutions."

This was fair comment on the persecuting spirit and uneasy alliances of the time. It was not easy to be impartial about the financial gains and losses of members of Parliament. Certainly the Commons often voted large sums of money to supporters .Lilburne asked, "Was a Parliament in England ever called for that end, as to rob and poll the poor common people...and then share it amongst the members of both houses?" But Lilburne did not hesitate to accept five farms in County Durham and even the sheriff's help to eject one of the tenants. Henry Marten's financial affairs would need an accountant to disentangle, but he was one of the biggest contributors of money to Parliament in its difficult days and may have advanced sums of up to £25,000 (i.e. between a quarter and half a million pounds in present day reckoning). There are records of repayments in 1649 of up to £3,600, but settlement dragged on and Henry exclaimed sarcastically "he had seen at last the Scripture fulfilled, - 'Thou hast exalted the humble and meek; thou hast filled the empty with good things, and the rich hast thou sent empty away!'"

On September 28th, Parliament gave him Leominster and other lands formerly belonging to the Duke of Buckingham as compensation for expenses and sums advanced. He visited these estates in 1650, for we find a record of 10s. "ffor wine and metheglin bestowed on Coll. Marten" at Leominster that year. The value of the estates still did not compensate for his "arrears due for serving Parliament as a soldier, and also for his good services to the commonwealth," and he was still applying to the Council of State in 1651.

X

After the defeat of the Levellers in the Army, Marten's irregular military career came to an end. On July 16th, 1649 "the well-affected gentry in South Wales pointed out that their commander-in-chief, Col. Horton, had been ordered to go to Ireland and suggested Henry Marten as a fit person to replace him. The House made no appointment until Sea-General Dawkins was sent down as one of Cromwell's regional Major-Generals. That summer everything possible was being done to raise money to pay the Army in Ireland, and on August 9th, Henry suggested selling the crown regalia for this purpose. No doubt the proposal was motivated less by an enthusiasm for the war in Ireland than by dislike of the royal trappings. His motion was adopted, and the King's jewels and other possessions were sold mainly to the courts of France, Spain, the Spanish Netherlands, and Sweden.

Henry Marten was able to get only one piece of Leveller legislation enacted, and even this was badly amended. The Levellers had always fought to humanise the treatment meted out to prisoners for debt, and on July 17th, 1649 Marten introduced a bill for Discharging Poor Prisoners. The debtors Marten wanted to help were not those guilty of fraud or deliberately obstructing justice, or the wealthy who obstinately refused to pay debts because they knew they could get privileged accommodation by bribing the gaoler, but the poor tradesmen who had borrowed capital and were themselves unable to recover sums owed to them to pay interest. These prisoners had no privileges and were thrown into filthy gaols, fed on scraps, ofter manacled, and not released until they had paid fees to the gaolers. The act was passed on September 4th, but unfortunately with an amendment which excluded all prisoners who had fought against Parliament.

In retrospect, it is clear that Marten's most important work in Parliament was the spread of ideas about tolerance. He proposed, though unsuccessfully, to repeal the statute of banishment made against the Jews in the years 1290 and declared himself in favour of tolerance for Catholics. Even for someone with parliamentary immunity, it was a time for caution, though this was not part of Henry's character. One member, offended by something Marten had said, proposed to expel all "profane and unsanctified persons" from the House. Henry rose and said, "That he should take the liberty to move, before the motion alluded to, that 'all fools might be put out likewise', and added, 'Then the House might probably be found thin enough'."

On May 14th, 1650 an act was passed "for suppressing the detestable sins of incest, adultery, and fornication," when Henry gave his opinion "That the severity of the Punishment by this Act, being death, would cause these Sins to be more frequently committed, because People would be more cautious in committing them for Fear of the Punishment, and being undiscovered, would be imboldened the more in the Commitment of them." Noble says that the following year, chiefly through Marten's efforts, the act was abrogated, from the fear he should be the first example of the severity of it, for "a more dissolute character it was impossible to find."

Henry threw his energies into committee work, and attended numerous meetings apparently because he hoped to be able to moderate decisions rather than to put them into force. For example, in June 1650 he was on the committee to suppress obscene and impious practices and the committee against atheistical and blasphemous opinions. On December 28th, the House considered a proposal to compel everybody to take the engagement to be faithful to the Commonwealth without a King or House of Lords, and to outlaw all persons who refused. The only modification of this tyrannical proposal was secured when Henry managed to substitute the word *men* for *persons* in one of the clauses and so saved women from persecution. As *Mercurius Pragmaticus* put it: "That lover of Mutton honest Harry Marten stood their friends, and breaking a Jest (in the Committee) said very merrily, Though they baited the Bull they would not baite the Cow too; and so that Clause of Women-subscribing was put out."

Henry Marten was particularly intersted in foreign affairs and he was a member of the Council of State's committees to consider foreign alliances, treaties with the United Provinces, and acts of hostility by the Dutch fleet; a member of the committee for Foreign Affairs, and a delegate to meet ambassadors. He spoke

French and probably Spanish and Italian. He was one of the committee which called on John Milton to invite him to become Secretary for the Foreign Languages. H.N. Brailsford has suggested that he may have been the member entrusted with French affairs. After the death of Cardinal Richelieu in 1642, the people of Bordeaux, who had had close links with England since the Middle Ages through the wine trade, followed the course of the Civil War with great interest, and there were even supporters of the Levellers there. It is known from surviving papers that between 1650 and 1652 Marten was receiving newsletters from Bordeaux, Paris and Saumur.

He was continually being sent by the Council of State to entertain foreign representatives, and he was certainly one of the few members at that time capable of combining diplomacy and conviviality. He entertained and negotiated with the ambassadors and envoys of Spain, Portugal, Denmark, Italy, the United Provinces and the State of Venice, and made no pretence that he shared the Puritanism of his colleagues. Harry took his mistress Mary Ward to at least one of these gatherings, for Sir Thomas Gower wrote on January 15th, 1652-3 : "Heert, the Spanish Ambassador, is discontented with the carriage of most of the English ladies who were at his entertainment, and they as much at him for giving the chief place and respect to Col. H. Martin's mistress...they are also much displeased at her for being finer and more bejewelled than any...'tis no small argument of the greatness of the Hogen Mogen Heeren Staten of England, that the Ambassador of the great monarch of Spain should make an entertainment for such a property belonging to one of the Parliament of England."

After 1649 it became difficult to write or publish any but official "news," and even the scandalous *Pragmaticus* ceased publication. A few stories of Henry Marten's activities survive. John Aubrey tells of his bitter attack on old Sir Henry Vane when he was voted off the Council in 1651. Marten ended his speech by saying, "But for young Sir Harry Vane..." and then sat down. Naturally some members called out, "What have you to say to young Sir Harry?" Marten rose and replied: "Why! if young Sir Harry lives to be old; he will be old Sir Harry!" Aubrey says this set the House laughing at a time when Vane was very powerful.

Another anecdote related by Aubrey referred to Marten's habit of pretending to sleep and "nod off" in the House as a hint to boring speakers. Alderman Atkins moved that such scandalous members as slept and minded not the business of the House should be put out. Marten rose to his feet and said, "Mr. Speaker, a motion has been made to turn out the nodders; I desire the noddies may also be turned out." Once during a debate Cromwell referred to *Sir* Harry Marten, whereupon Marten rose and bowed: "I thank your Majesty! I always thought when you were King that I should be knighted."

After Cromwell's victories at Drogheda and Wexford, Henry foresaw that Oliver had acquired an authority which could lead to dictatorship. In the House he said, "If they were to be governed by a single person, their last king would have been as proper a gentleman for it as any in England, for he found no fault with his person, but his office only." Anthony à Wood said Marten's speeches "were not long but wondrous poynant, pertinent and witty. He was exceedingly happy in apt instances; he alone hath sometimes turned the whole House." The time for speeches was nearing the end.

The republicans were anxious to prevent military dictatorship and saw themselves as the guardians of the new government. Henry Marten compared the Commonwealth to the infant Moses. When the baby found in the ark among the bulrushes was taken to Pharoah's daughter, she took care to find the child's own mother to nurse it and bring it up. The Commonwealth was still an infant "of a weak growth and a very tender constitution," and Henry said his opinion was "that nobody would be so fit to nurse it as the mother who brought it forth, and that they should not think of putting it under any other hands until it had obtained more years and vigour."

The Rump Parliament survived for another two years, accomplishing very few of the reforms they had fought for. On April 20th, 1653 Cromwell decided the time had come to expel the members by force. According to Dugdale, "attended with strong Guards, he entered the Parliament-House (with Fleetwood his great Confident) commanding some few of his attendants to tarry without. Where, without moving his Hat, or going to any seat, he first addressed his speech to the Chief Justice St. John; telling him, that he then came to do that which grieved him to the very Soul and what he had earnestly, with Tears, pray'd to God against. Nay, that he had rather be torn in pieces than do it: But, that there was a Necessity laid upon him therein, in order to the Glory of God, and the good of this Nation."

He then turned towards the Speaker and told him that Parliament had "upon their own Pride and Luxury, consum'd the wealth of the Land. Which being said he gave a stamp with his Feet, and bad them for shame be gone, and give place to honester men." He walked up and down in a rage and shouted out, "You are no Parliament; I will put an end to your sitting." He called in some of the musketeers and gave orders for the Speaker to be pulled out of his chair. Pointing to the mace he said, "What shall we do with this bauble? here, take it away." As the members left Cromwell abused them. "It was observed, that as they went out of the House, he pointed at Harry Marten and Tom Challonor; and said, Is it fit that such fellows as these, Should sit to Govern? Men of vicious Lives; the one a noted Whore-Master,and the other a Drunkard?"

A government of "saints" was chosen by the Council of the Army from a list of names submitted by the Independent churches of each county. Known as the Barebones Parliament after one of its members, it ruled from July 4, until it was dissolved by Major-General Lamert's musketeers on December 12th. Four days later Lambert and the Army drew up what they called the Instrument of Government which provided for Cromwell as Lord Protector to be head of the Executive, Army, and Navy with power to issue ordinances when Parliament was not sitting. Cromwell's first Protectorate Parliament lasted for five months. On July 12th, 1654 Marten wrote from the Holy Lambe in Abingdon that he was going to Beckett, his Berkshire home, and "they are now chusing Knights of ye shire in the market place."

By this time Marten and his friends could meet in taverns or private houses, but had no access to the press or any contact with the general public. John Wildman arrested on February 12th, 1654-5 for opposition to Cromwell, and Henry Marten may have been imprisoned for debt at about the same time. He was outlawed in January, but may not have been actually taken until later. In the Berkshire Record Office there is a copy of *Gallen's New Almanack* for 1655 with notes by Henry Marten throughout the year which seem to indicate that he was still at liberty. He notes visits to his "brattes" i.e. Mary Ward's children, the purchase of gifts for his daughter, "propositions for discharging my debts and if that take not, about selling my land everywhere ...if not that neither, get leave of my creditors to be at liberty for 1 year go speedily about setling my estate...Turn ye dining-room at ye new house into lodging for our own family. Visit Mrs. Holland and ask for my furred coat," and so on. In May he had a Memo to meet a Mr. Brompton at the Globe Inn in Fleet Street. In October he went to Oxford and his Berkshire houses and then made a brief visit to Leominster.

On August 20th, 1656 another general election took place, but although there was a good deal of republican opposition to Cromwell, even the leaders who did get elected were excluded from Parliament. Henry Marten was up to his neck in debts and, with the help of his royalist brother-in-law Lord Lovelace, struggling to keep out of a debtor's prison. If he was confined at this time it was probably in the Rules at Southwark, where he would be able to get privileged treatment and keep in touch with his friends. That year James Harrington published his *Commonwealth of Oceana* advocating the ancient classical type of republicanism, and Henry Marten wrote some notes which he considered printing as a commentary on Harrison's ideas. He was certainly in prison in the Rules on May 5th, 1657.

Henry's brother George wrote to him from Barbadoes asking him to help George's daughter Susan to go out to him. Henry's daughter wrote to thank her father for some money ("It will not goe very far but a lettle is better than nothing"). His son Henry wrote to ask for a laced coat and to "help his Master to some pupils." The constables of St. George's Parish, Southwark asked him to pay "the bearer 5s. for watching for him 15 nights in 15 months, at 4d. per night" - the request dated March 1st. 1657-8 may indicate how long Henry had been in the Rules.

XI

Oliver Cromwell died on September 3rd. 1658 and his son Richard was proclaimed Protector. Addresses of congratulation poured in from all over the country, but the republicans hoped for a revival of their fortunes. Letters from John Wildman to Henry Marten hint at some sort of plot. They were still using a code which they had elaborated years before, with O for Marten, A for Wildman, L for Cromwell, N for Ireton, X for Fairfax, and so on. On January 11th. Marten's agent, Thomas Deane, wrote from Leominster about the coming elections, which Richard Cromwell had been forced to hold in order to get funds. "Here is a very great dicision and much seakinge, the Burgimasters playing their game variously, and the rest of the towns the licke. They are so compounded and so divided that although it might seeme so much the more hopefull yet it is so much the more uncertaine, insomuch that the best of my witts invitts mee not to begge, hunt, or crave with much earnestnesse, but only to make it knowen that if their loue bee so much towards you as to make choyce of you, that you will bee willing to serue them." The election took place without Henry, but the republicans became a strong minority in the House.

Henry was desperate to be released from Southwark. As long as Oliver was in power he probably felt safer in the Rules and did not think it advisable to buy his release by selling his mortgaged estates. But on March 1st. 1659 he offered the manor of Hartington in Derbyshire for sale for £9,500 and on March 22nd. for £9,000. The Army leaders supported the republicans and refused to recognize Richard Cromwell as Protector. In order to avoid another civil war, Richard dissolved Parliament on April 21st. and resigned the following month. On May 2nd. John Wildman, Henry Marten, Samuel Moyer, Henry Nevile, John Lawson, and John Jones published *The Armies Dutie*, with an introduction stating that they had written two letters to Lord Fleetwood offering advice, without any intention to publish, but since he had ignored them they were now making their own views public. They warned Fleetwood against setting up a monarchy: "The very essence or formal reason of a Nations freedom, consists in the peoples making their own Lawes and Magistrates, and therefore it is a contradiction to say, we are free under a Prince controlling our Lawes in their Creation, or Execution, and imposing his Officers upon us at his will."

Fleetwood and the Council of Officers decided to invite back to Parliament members who had supported the "Good Old Cause" between 1648 and 1653. Dugdale says that on May 7th. the members came to the Painted Chamber, "but finding of their designed number (which was forty and two) that there wanted a couple, they sent to the Gaols for a present supply." The tract *Englands Confusion* reported that Parliament "sent for the two chaste cock sparrows, the Lord Munson and Mr. Henry Martin, out of prison, where they were in execution of debt." Henry was at once selected to draw up a declaration to the people and to become a member of the committee to consider the administration of justice. John Aubrey says, "Henry Martyn made a motion in the house to call the *addressers* to account (viz. those that addressed to Richard Cromwell, Protector, to stand by him with their lives and fortunes,) and that all the addressers that were of the house might be turn'd out as enemies to the commonwealth of England and betrayers of their trust to bring in government by a single person. Had not Dick Cromwell sneak't away, then it is certaine that the Rump would have cut-off his head."

For a short time Henry Marten was one of the disillusioned members of the former Long Parliament who governed England with the support of the Army. He moved into Whitehall and did some small services such as preventing the sale of Somerset House chapel "because it was the place of meeting for the French church." For a couple of months the Army again prevented Parliament from sitting until General Monk entered England from Scotland with 6,000 men and declared himself in favour of restitution. Opinion in the country was divided between hostility to military government and scorn for the Rump Parliament.

Monk advanced towards London as the champion of Parliament against militarism, and few of the members realised his real intentions until it was too late. Ludlow and Marten had forbodings, and the former wrote: "In his march he removed many officers from their commands, placing in their room persons of ruined fortune or profligate lives, making no distinction between those that had continued in their obedience to the Parliament, and those who had declared against them...Wherein his deportment was so visible, that Col. Martin in the Parliament House resembled him to one, that being sent for to make a sute of clothes, brought with him a budget full of carpenter's tools, and being told that such things were not at all fit for the work he was desired to do, answered, 'it matters not, I will do your work well enough, I warrant you'."

General Monk reached London on February 3rd. and found the City was strongly opposed to the Rump. On February 13th. Parliament voted to be true to the Engagement, but on February 21st. Monk restored the expelled Presbyterians who soon rescinded every act carried since 1648, arranged for a Convention Parliament to meet, and dissolved itself on March 16th. Monk then opened negotiations with Charles II, who issued the Declaration of Breda in which he promised an amnesty for everybody not excluded by Parliament. Charles II entered London on May 29th.

On June 1st. a proclamation called upon the "regicides" to surrender, but its ambiguity caused some to believe that surrender would ensure their liberty. Because of this "An Act of Free and General Pardon, Indemnity, and Oblivion" was passed on June 6th. which excepted by name certain men who were to be proceeded against as "Traitors to his late Majesty, according to the Laws of England, and are out of this present Act wholly excepted." Paragraphs XXXV and XXXVI of the Act named Henry Marten and others as having personally appeared according to the Proclamation "and do pretend thereby to some Favour, upon some conceived doubtful Words in the said Proclamation," so that if they should be sentenced to death their execution would be suspended until an Act of Parliament could be passed for that purpose.

There was a feeling of terror among republicans. Lucy Hutchinson wrote: "The Presbyterians were now the white boys, and according to their nature fell a thirsting, and then hunting after blood, urging that God's blessing could not be upon the land, till justice had cleansed it from the late king's blood." At first the prisoners were held at Lambeth House, where Lucy Hutchinson said she saw Monk and his wife come to the garden "and caused them to be brought down only to stare at them, which was a barbarism, for that man, who had betrayed so many poor men to death and misery that never hurt him, but who had honoured him." On August 24th. they were delivered to the Lieutenant of the Tower to await trial.

Henry Marten's papers were seized and some of his letters came into the hands of Edmund Gayton, who published them as *Familiar Letters to his Lady of Delight*. The lady was Mary Ward, Henry's de facto wife, for he had been separated from his legal wife, "the old lady at Longworth," for many years. In the first of the letters Henry wrote: "I might well employ some time in arraigning my selfe at the bar of my own conscience, and finde, if I could, how I came to deserve (from men I mean) the rigours I undergo in the losse of that reputation and estate I left behind me."

He continued: "The report of the crimes charged upon me overtakes me wheresoever I go, though the reporters know not how nearly some of their auditors are concerned therein...Could I have foreseen how dearly publicke freedome must be bought, and how hardly it can be kept, I would have used onely my passive valour against all the late Kings oppressions, rather than voted, as I did, any War at all, though a defensive one...Had I suspected that the Axe which took off the late Kings head, should have been made a stirrop for our first false General, I should sooner have consented to my owne death then his."

On October 9th. 1660 the 29 regicides were formally indicted at Hicks Hall, the sessions-house of the Middlesex justices. Lord Chief Baron Sir Orlando Bridgman presided. The following day the prisoners were taken in several coaches guarded by men on horse and on foot to Newgate, and from there to the Old Bailey. Three of the prisoners unsuccessfully tried to avoid committing themselves to a plea of guilty or not guilty. Then Henry Marten and five others were brought before the court. The account of the trial records the preliminary skirmishing.

Clerk. Henry Martin, how sayest thou? Art thou guilty of the Treason, whereof thou standest Indicted, and art now Arraigned? or Not guilty?

Marten. I desire the benefit of the Act of Oblivion -

Clerk. Are you Guilty? or Not guilty?

Court. You are to understand, the Law is this, the same to you, and everyone; You are to plead Guilty, or Not guilty. If you will demand the benefit of the Act of Oblivion, it is a confession of being Guilty.

Marten. I humbly conceive the Act of Indemnity -

Court. You must plead Guilty or Not guilty.

Marten. If I plead I lose the benefit of that Act.

Court. You are totally excepted out of the Act.

Marten. If it were so I would plead. My name is not in that Act.

Court. Henry Martin is there.

Mr. Solicitor General. Surely he hath been kept close prisoner indeed, if he hath not seen the Act of Indemnity. Shew it him...

Marten. Henry Martin? My name is not so: it is Harry Marten.

The Solicitor-General quoted the precedent of a man named Baxter which had been written as Bagster and "adjudged all one," and after the judge had ruled the misnomer could not be given in evidence Henry pleaded not guilty.

Thomas Harrison was the first to be tried, found guilty, and hanged, drawn and quartered. Evelyn records in his *Diary* the execution of some of the regicides at Charing Cross "in sight of the place where they put to death their natural prince, and in the presence of the King his son, whom they also sought to kill. I saw not their execution, but met their quarters, mangled, and cut, and reeking, as they were brought from the gallows in baskets on the hurdle."

Marten's trial took place at the Old Bailey on October 16th. His name was called with the charge: "He did both Sign and Seal the Precept for Summoning the Court, and the Warrant for Execution; sat almost every day, and particularly the Day of Sentence." Henry replied that he did not dispute the matter of of fact, "the Malice set aside, Maliciously, Murderously, and Traitorously."

The Lord Chief Baron would not accept this, and argued, "If a Man meet another in the Street, and run him through, in this Case the Law implies Malice; though but to an ordinary Watchman, there is Malice by the Law in the fact; if there was no such expressed Personal Malice as you conceive, yet the Fact done implies Malice in Law." Marten protested that there was no fact "that is a Crime in itself, but as it is Circumstantiated," and the judge agreed that "all Actions are circumstantiated," but the killing of the King is Treason of all Treasons."

The Counsel for the prosecution intervened to say he would prove malice by bringing a witness to say Marten "was in great Sport at the time of the Signing of the Warrant," and a former servant named Ewer described how Cromwell and Marten had inked each other. Sir Purbeck Temple deposed that he had hidden in the Painted Chamber and heard Cromwell ask by what authority the King should be tried, to which Marten replied, "In the Name of the Commons and Parliament assembled, and all the good People of England."

Henry did not deny this, but told the Court that the Commission went in the name of the Commons assembled in Parliament "and what a Matter is it for one of the Commissioners to say, Let it be acted by the Good People of England?" To this the Solicitor General retorted, "You know all Good People did abhor it; I am sorry to see so little Repentance."

"My Lord," said Marten, "if it were possible for that Blood to be in the Body again, and every Drop that was shed in the late Wars, I could wish it with all my Heart: But, my Lord, I hope it is Lawful to offer in my Defence that, which, when I did it, I thought I might do. My Lord, there was the House of Commons, as I understood it, (perhaps your Lordships think it was not a House of Commons,) but it was the Supream Authority of England; it was so reputed both at Home and Abroad."

He was fighting for his life, and the legal quibbles could end in disembowelling and hacking of limbs, but he could not resist a reminder that he never supported the theory of the divine right of kings. "I think his Majesty that now is is King upon the best Title under Heaven, for he was called in by the Representative Body of England." This was too much for the Solicitor-General, who commented that he must have an answer in Parliament to that speech. Marten said he confessed that he adhered to the Parliament's Army heartily, but his qualified expression did not please the Court.

The jury found all the prisoners guilty. Ten were condemned to death, and were hanged, drawn and quartered. The rest were sent to the Tower to await Parliament's decision about their execution.

Great Seal of the Commonwealth.

Reproduced from Lord Brougham's *Old England's Worthies*.

Interior of the Old Bailey during the trial of the Regicides, 1660.
(By courtesy of the Trustees of the British Museum.)

XII

In the early days of November it was generally expected that Henry Marten would be hanged with another regicide, Col. Robert Tichborne, but it turned out that Tichborne had saved the life of the Lieutenant of the Tower and a vintner in Cornhill, and both petitioned for the execution to be deferred. Henry wrote to Mary Ward asking her to find out what the Court was thinking ("As White-hall pipes, Westminster will dance") and to get a friend to hear the sermon preached before the King, as "something might be pick'd out of it." He was anxious to discover if he was "in the black book," and observed that "God does use to acquaint his Ambassadors with much of his mind." On another occasion he reassured her: "I shall now give some comfort to thy little heart, having lately perused the Kings speech and the Chancelors, either I am very much mistaken in them, or they signified no great danger to us, whose faults are almost as old as ourselves."

His estates were seized on November 28th. but in any case they were mortgaged to the extent of £30,000. His financial affairs were in complete chaos, and some of the property was apparently acquired by Lord Lovelace, who had gone surety for him. John Loder, who had bought Henry's manor of Hinton in 1658, visited him in the Tower, where he discussed with some anxiety other financial arrangements they had made. Henry Marten told Mary that Loder "knew not whether he should be undone or no by meddling with my estate; they bear him down at Court that all is juggling betixt him and me." In the end it was decided that the allowance of £2 a week that Marten was getting through Loder's cousin Stanton would in future be paid by Henry's sister, Elizabeth Edmonds, now a widow.

On January 26th. 1660-1, the bodies of Cromwell and Ireton were dug up from their graves in Westminster Abbey, and four days later, with the carcase of Bradshaw, they were taken to Tyburn and hanged. Then their heads were stuck on poles and the rest of their bodies thrown into a pit beneath the gallows. Reflecting on the temper of Parliament, Henry wrote to Mary Ward: "Tomorrow morning we are all to appear at the House of

Commons to shew cause why the sentence given against us should not be executed." Later he wrote: "I was told on Tuesday night, that the House of Commons had given us all up...Look upon my little brats, and see if thy Deare be not among them; has not one of 'um his face, another his braines, another his mirth? And look thou most upon that, for it is just the best thing in this world, and a thing that could not be taken from me, when Lemster was, when all the remainder of my Estate and thine was; nor when my liberty and the assurance of my life was, and when thy company was."

On February 20th. Marten appeared before the House of Lords, with no apologies for the political actions which had brought him there. But being asked why he should not be executed, he replied, "That honourable House of Commons, that he did so idolise, had given him up to death, and now this honourable House of Peers, which he had so much opposed, especially in their power of judicature, was made the sanctuary for him to flee to for life."

Lord Falkland, remembering the jest by which Henry had saved Sir William Davenant, said, "Gentlemen, yee talke here of making a sacrifice; it was old lawe, all sacrifices were to be without spot or blemish; and now you are going to make an old rotten rascal a sacrifice." Some of the lords probably laughed, some must have recalled that Marten had often intervened to save the lives of royalists, and it was "concluded in the end, he should rot out the remainder of his life in the gaol."

In the Tower everyone was in fear of the Lieutenant, Sir John Robinson, but when he was drunk, and particularly when he was absent altogether, the rules were relaxed. Henry told Mary that the Gentleman Porter was good to him and that he allowed him to walk once a day "on top of his leads." One day he was even allowed into the Gentleman Porter's lodgings "and tickled his Gooseberry-bushes." Henry's keeper was "very civil" to him, but he was "just the worst Keeper in the Tower for keeping times." All the prisoners were unlocked before 7 a.m., but Henry was always locked up until at least 8 a.m. and sometimes 10 a.m. He took this philosophically, but his late release meant he could not get to the Tower food-stalls until the best was gone.

He bought food from his allowance to send to Mary Ward and the children, and sometimes she was able to send food and drink in to him. He mentions in his letters sending "a piece of butter, such as is brought into the Tower," "two Tower loaves of two sorts, and every pennie of money I have," and "a leg of mutton, two loaves, a peck of flower (though not of 18d. the bushel) and four bottles of Will Parkers Lemon Ale."

Henry's daughters sometimes visited him, but not his wife, "the Old Woman at Longworth." Three of his daughters, Anne, Jane and Rebecca, lived at Longworth with their mother. Frances was married to William Pryor of Longworth. Elizabeth married George Spyller, who is mentioned in one of Henry's letters as being "sworn a Privy-chamber man extraordinary, which is worth little to him more then the protecting him from arrests." Mary, who was called by her father affectionately "Mall," was married to Thomas Parker, who later became the 2nd. Lord Morley and Mounteagle. These two were his favourites. His only son Henry or Hal was a young man of twenty at the time of the arrest; and lived an uneventful life at Longworth, where he became a church-warden in 1681.

Whatever truth there may have been in the Royalist naming of Harry's numerous mistresses, since at least the time of the notorious party at the Spanish Ambassador's he had regarded Mary as his wife and given her the name of Marten. He advised her, "If an officer come that thou thinkest is one indeed, thou must give him thy right name; thou maist tell him thy other too, and bid him set down both, for thou art known and called by both." They had three children, Peggy, Sarah (known as Poppet), and the baby Henrietta (called Bacon-Hog). At the time of the baby's birth Henry had Sarah in the Tower with him, and he wrote, "How pitifully Sarah cries now she is with her father."

Mary tried to visit him, and he replied, "The danger thou wert in by coming to me, and the fright I was in by telling me so: for the simple woman when she was denied coming into the Tower, and delivered her basket and napkin at the gate, must needs tell them she had a letter too for the Collonel: which, by good fortune, though the other broke it open, no body read it but the Gentleman Porter, and he told them there was nothing in it, as indeed there was not, but about the little girle: yet that might have bred trouble enough, as it was like to have been construed; and the Gentleman Porter himself does not know how it may be taken if she should stay long; she's shod but wants other things pitifully." He added, "Since I wrote thus far, Master T... advises me to rid away the girle so soon as ever I can conveniently, for the strictness increases."

At last there was the opportunity for a visit, probably during the absence in the country of the Lieutenant of the Tower. Henry sent Mary detailed instructions what to do. "First thou art to make a rogue of thy self, then to take what guard thou wilt to the water side, then a boat at what stairs thou wilt...to be at the by-ward about one of the clock, and then come in the crowd, but without thy brother or thy friend, or anybody that has been seen with thee: no body will take notice of thee here, but one, that stands there on purpose to bring thee off, if need be. In case thou hast a couple of Squires to conduct thee so far, thou may'st direct them to retire to the Angel or the Rose, or some such good-neighbouring place, or perhaps to Gardiners or Mother Thorntons within the Tower, and yet keep distance enough from thee; and we shall be able to send them their dinner in victuals, their drink, thou knowest, is to be called for at their quarters, and that (being moderate) will be cleared too. Whether thou wilt take this opportunity of bringing the poor girl along with thee, I leave to thy discretion."

The meeting took place without detection, and was followed by a few others when the Lieutenant was "dining abroad." But the meetings soon came to an end. Henry made arrangements for Mary's belongings to be taken to the house of his daughter Mary Parker, and advised her to follow by coach. "Till thou goest into the country, thou must not trust to any lodging too long, notwithstanding thy change of habit." Above all she must get away from London, he told her, and added hopefully, "I presume I shall obtain leave for a sight of thee once at least before thou goest."

A Traytors head.

Execution of the Regicides, October 1660, from *A True and Perfect Relation of the Grand Traytors Execution.*

Chepstow Castle drawn by I. Kip, 1705 (from Atkyns's *Gloucestershire*, 1712)
"Marten's Tower" is the one nearest to the bridge in this engraving

XIII

Lucy Hutchinson wrote bitterly that when imprisonment did not kill the regicides fast enough "and when some alms were thus privately stolen into them, they were sent away to remote and dismal islands, where relief could not reach them, nor any of their relations take care of them." A warrant from Hampton Court dated July 25th, 1662 ordered Sir John Robinson, Lieutenant of the Tower, to deliver Henry Marten into the custody of Capt. James Lambert of the *Anne* for transportation to Berwick. He and Col. Tichborne (who died in the Tower in 1682) were placed in the custody of William, 1st. Baron Widdrington at Berwick, an ironical situation for Henry who had formerly so strongly opposed both the Scots and the Earl of Northumberland. He once wrote to Mary Ward, "I have beene on bare boord a thousand times in my life, and yet still found a twig or something to hold me up." He may even have had some hope still, for it was alleged on October 15th, 1663 that he was receiving correspondence from one of John Wildman's men.

On May 19th, 1665 three warrants were issued to "deliver at Holy Island, convey, and receive at Windsor Castle, Henry Martin, prisoner for the horrid murder of the late King." It is not known why he and Tichborne were removed, but a pamphleteer alleged that "an Honest blunt Scotch Knight understanding they were remov'd for better Air, plainly told the King, they thought the Isle of Wight Air good enough for his Father, and the worst Air in Hell was too good for such rogues as they." On December 7th, 1668 a warrant was issued to Prince Rupert, the Constable of Windsor Castle, to have Marten conveyed to Chepstow.

As a state prisoner, Henry Marten was housed in a large room about 36 feet by 23 feet, in the tower which now bears his name in Chepstow castle. There was a local tradition that he had two servants, Catherine and Margaret Vick, who lived in the upper room, but there is no reliable information about his life as a prisoner. Anthony à Wood said he "lived very poor, and in shabbed condition in his confinement, and would be glad to take a pot of ale from any one that would give it to him." There is an anecdote that he was allowed to walk out to St. Pierre to visit the Lewis family, but this originated in a letter written by the Dean of Exeter as late as July 26th, 1768. Thomas Lewis is said to have asked Marten whether he would sign the death warrant if he had his life over again, and when Henry replied that he would, he was told never to visit St. Pierre again.

Marten's prisons seem to have been selected by someone with a sense of irony, for Chepstow castle had for a time been the property of Oliver Cromwell before being returned to the Marquis of Worcester, who was himself suspected of treason. In 1678 Titus Oates and the Chepstow-born William Bedloe alleged that the Marquis was one of the people involved in a Popish plot to burn down the City of London. It was argued that "the garrison of Chepstow be disbanded, and the arms removed, and the castle demolisht, it having alwaies bin in ill hands." What a pity there is no record of the comments of the 'Roman pagan' as he watched the Catholic Marquis's garrison scrupulously marched to church every Sunday!

Henry Marten died on September 9th, 1680, as Wood says, "with meat in his mouth, that is suddenly, in Chepstow Castle." He was buried in the chancel of Chepstow church, probably with the minimum of ceremony, but with many curious onlookers. In the parish register a portion of the page has been cut out where the entry of his burial must have been written. John Aubrey wrote of him: "He was a great and faithful lover of his countrey. He was of an incomparable witt for repartees; not at all covetous; humble, not at all arrogant, as most of them were; a great cultor of justice, and did always in the house take the part of the oppressed."

Appendix: His Epitaph

The acrostic epitaph Marten is supposed to have written himself may have been composed by someone who provided a tombstone after the Revolution of 1688-9. It has been said that the Rev. Thomas Chest, who became Vicar of Chepstow in 1702, was a royalist and removed Henry's body from the chancel to the "passage leading from the nave into the north aisle, nearly opposite the reading desk." The remains of the central tower of the church fell down in 1703, so Thomas Chest may not have had any political motive for re-interring the body. In 1768 a visitor recorded that the "epitaph in ye church is effaced by being on ye floor, and very few persons remember it." A new stone was cut to replace this with modernized lettering, and a third stone now lies inside the church near the West door. (There may have been one more replacement, and this or the second stone is in Chepstow Museum). The lettering is partly effaced, and there are slight differences in the recorded copies, but the following is probably the best version:

Here
Was buried a true Englishman
Who in Berkshire was well known
To love his country's freedom 'bove his own,
But living immured full twenty year
Had time to write as doth appear
His Epitaph.
Here or elsewhere, all's one to you, or me,
Earth, air, or water grips my ghostless dust,
None knows how soon to be by fire set free.
Reader, if you an oft tried rule will trust,
You'll gladly do and suffer what you must.
My life was spent with serving you and you,
And death's my pay, it seems, and welcome, too;
Revenge destroying but itself, while I
To birds of prey leave my old cage and fly.
Examples preach to the eye; care then (mine says)
Not how you end but how you spend your days.

Bibliography

A full list of sources would take up a disproportionate space in a book of this length, so the following short-title list is a compromise. London publication unless stated otherwise. E references are to Thomason Tracts.

Ashley, M.: *Greatness of Oliver Cromwell*, 1957.

Abbott, W. C. & C. D. Crane: *Writings and Speeches of Oliver Cromwell*, 2 vols. 1937-9, Harvard and Cambridge.

Ashmole, E.: *Antiquities of Berkshire*, 1736 (1st. 1719).

Aubrey, J.: *Brief Lives*, Oxford, 1898, ed. A. Clark; 1958 ed. O. L. Dick; 1949 ed. A. Powell. *Lives of Eminent Men*, 1813.

Baker, A.: *Historic Abingdon*, Abingdon, 1965.

(Baron, W.:) *Regicides no Saints nor Martyrs*, 1700.

Berkshire Record Office: M.S. Diary in *Gallen's New Almanack*, 1655, D-ELs-F18.

Brailsford, H.N.: *The Levellers*, ed. C. Hill, 1961.

Carlyle, T.: *Letters and Papers of Oliver Cromwell*, 1845-6.

Catermole, R.: *The Great Civil War*, 1841-4.

Clarendon, Edward Hyde, Earl of: *Calendar of the Clarendon State Papers*, Oxford, 1869-1932; *History of the Rebellion and Civil Wars*, Oxford, 1702-4; *Life*, 1759.

Cobbet, W.: *Parliamentary History*, 1806-20.

Cole, Mrs. J.C.: *Notes on Marten* in Berks. Arch. Soc. Jnl. No. 49, 1946.

D'Ewes, Sir S.: *Journal; and* BM Harleian MSS. 162-5.

Dugdale, Sir W.: *Short View of the Late Troubles*, Oxford, 1681.

Firth, C.H.: *Henry Marten* in D.N.B.; *Oliver Cromwell and the Rule of the Puritans*, 1901; *Last Years of the Protectorate*, 1909; ed. *The Clarke Papers*, 4 vols. 1891-1901; (with R.S. Rait) ed. *Acts and Ordinances of the Interregnum*, 1911; (with G. Davies) ed. *Regimental History of Cromwell's Army*, Oxford, 1940.

Forster, J.: *Eminent British Statesmen*, 1838.

Frank, J.: *The Levellers*, Harvard, 1955.

Gardiner, S. R.: *History of the Great Civil War*, 1888-91; *History of the Commonwealth and Protectorate*, 1894-1901; *Fall* of the Monarchy, 1882; History of England, 1887-90.

Godwin, W.:   History of the Commonwealth, 1824-8.

Gregg, P.:   Free-born John, 1961.

Heylin, P.:   History of the Presbyterians, Oxford, 1672.

Hexter, J.H.:   Reign of King Pym, Harvard, 1941.

Hill, C.:   The English Revolution, 1940, 1955; Puritanism and Revolution, 1958; (with E. Dell) ed. The Good Old Cause, 1949.

Hill, E.F.:   Parish of Shrivenham, Faringdon, 1928.

Historical Manuscripts Commission: Reports, particularly 13th., App. IV, 1892, Loder-Symonds; App. I, Portland; Reports 1,2,4,5,6,9.

Hutchinson, L.:   Memoirs of Col. Hutchinson, 1846 (5th.).

Ireland, W.W.:   Sir Henry Vane, 1905.

Journals of the House of Commons and House of Lords.

Keeler, M.F.:   Long Parliament, Philadelphia, 1954.

Lilburne, J.:   Letters to Marten E.407(41), 669. f. 11(46); Rash Oaths Unwarrantable, E.393(39); Legall Fundamentall Liberties, etc.

Ludlow, E.:   Memoirs, 1698 (ed. C.H. Firth, Oxford, 1894).

Marten, Henry: Three Speeches delivered at a Common-Hall, July 28th, 1643, E.63(8); The Interest of England Maintained, June 8th, 1646, E.340(5) and 669. f. 10(58); A Corrector of the Answerer to the Speech out of Doores, Oct. 26th, 1646, Edinburgh, E.364(9); A Word to Mr. Wil. Prynn, Esq., Jan. 6th, 1649, E.537(16) The Parliaments Proceedings Justified, Feb. 7th, 1648, E.425(20x); The Independency of England Endeavoured to be Maintained, Jan. 11th, 1648, E.422(16); (?) Englands Troublers Troubled, Aug. 17th, 1648, and Vox Plebis, Nov. 19th, 1646, E.362(20); Familiar Letters, edns. 1662-85; (?) with Overton and Walwyn, Remonstrance of Many Thousand Citizens, July 7th, 1646; (with Wildman and others) : The Armies Dutie, May 2nd, 1659, E.980(12).

Maseres, F.:   Select Tracts, 2 vols. 1815.

Money, W.:   Battles of Newbury, 2nd. ed. 1884.

Noble, M.:   Lives of the English Regicides, 1798

Pearl, V.:   London and the Outbreak of the Puritan Revolution, Oxford 1960.

Pease, T.C.:   Leveller Movement, Washington 1916.

Rushworth, J.:   Historical Collections, 1659-80.

Ryves, W.:   Newes of Dennington, March 26th, 1646, E.330(13)

Scott, Sir W. ed.:   Somers Tracts, 13 vols. 1809-15.

Thomason Tracts in British Museum. Catalogue, 1908. Numerous pamphlets, posters, and newsbooks.

Turvil, W.: *Terrible and bloudy Newes*, 1648, E.462(28).

Whitaker, L.: *Diary* in BM Addnl. MSS. 31116, fols.65,66v, 70v,71.

Whitelocke, Sir B.: *Memorials of English Affairs*, 1682.

Woodhouse, A.S.P.: *Puritanism and Liberty*, 1938.

Walker, C.: *History of Independency*, 1648, 1660.

Wedgewood, C.V.: *The King's War*, 1949.

Wolfe, Don M.: *Leveller Manifestoes*, Edinburgh, 1944.

Wood, A. *Athenae Oxonienses*, 5 vols. 1813-20.

Yule, G.: *Independents in the Civil War*, Cambridge, 1958.

PRO: *Calendar of State Papers, Domestic; Calendar of Treasury Books. Exact and Impartial Account of the Trial of 29 Regicides*, 1660.

Statutes at Large, 1735.

Brotherton Library, Leeds: Loder-Symonds papers, letters June 1652 and May 5th, 1657.

Newsbooks in the BM Thomason Collection, particularly *Mercurius Aulicus, Mercurius Elencticus;* and *Mercurius Pragmaticus.* Other newsbooks in this collection and also in Cardiff Central Library: *Kingdomes Weekly Intelligencer, Mercurius Bellicus, Mercurius Dogmaticus, Mercurius Melancholicus, Mercurius Rusticus, Parliament-Kite,* etc.

Index